Vanunu's WAIT for LIBERTY

REMEMBERING
The USS LIBERTY
And My Life
as a Candidate
of Conscience for
US HOUSE 2012

Eileen Fleming

Order this book online at www.trafford.com
or email orders@trafford.com

Most Trafford titles are also available at major online book retailers.

Cover art by Ben Negrete

Printed in the United States of America.

ISBN: 978-1-4669-7055-7 (sc)
ISBN: 978-1-4669-7054-0 (e)

Trafford rev. 12/06/2012

 www.trafford.com

North America & international
toll-free: 1 888 232 4444 (USA & Canada)
phone: 250 383 6864 ♦ fax: 812 355 4082

Is dedicated to the crew, family and friends of the USS LIBERTY and to the career and spirit of Journalist Helen Thomas.

"Remember, Remember the 5th of November. I suddenly had this feeling that everything is connected. Perfectly laid out in front of me and we are all a part of it and trapped by it. IDEAS are bulletproof."

Today is the 5th of November 2012. As I began the editing for my fourth book, that quote from "V for Vendetta" came to me as I also recalled the last line I wrote in my third book, "BEYOND NUCLEAR: Mordechai Vanunu's FREEDOM of SPEECH Trial and My Life as a Muckraker: 2005-2010" which reads, "And the bottom line for me is that experience is not just what happens to you, but what you do with it and que sera sera."

IF only Israel had been just and merciful in 2004, '05, '06, '07, '08, '09, '10, '11, or 2012; and allowed Vanunu his right to leave Israel, I IMAGINE that my fourth book would NOT be titled, "Vanunu's WAIT for LIBERTY, Remembering the USS LIBERTY and My Life as a candidate of Conscience for US HOUSE 2012."

"You must give birth to your images [IMAGINATION]. They are the future waiting to be born. Fear not the strangeness you feel. The future must enter you long before it happens."-Rainer Maria Rilke

That was the quote that came to me while I was writing my first book—"KEEP HOPE ALIVE"—which was inspired by the life and memories of a 1948 Palestinian Muslim refugee entwined with my spiritual journey that became very political during my first of seven trips to both sides of The Wall in Israel Palestine.

1

It has been said that if you are not crazy before you get to Jerusalem-you will go crazy there.

One crazy image that I committed to dreaming began during my first of seven trips to Jerusalem in 2005. I also vowed it aloud to Vanunu that I would write his saga UNTIL Israel allows its nuclear whistle blower the right to leave the state and "have a job, a home, a family" which is all he has wanted since he emerged from 18 years in a windowless tomb sized cell on April 21, 2004.

The crazy dream to run for US HOUSE of Representatives came to me shortly after establishing the public service website,www.WeAreWideAwake. org. On July 22, 2005, which was three weeks after my first trip to both sides of The Wall in Israel Palestine.

A few days before this writing, while I was cleaning out a window seat I stumbled upon five photos that I had stashed inside of a stack of literature from 2005, 2006 and 2007 trips to Israel Palestine. In the midst of throwing it all out, the forgotten photos I shot in east Jerusalem spilled out. I had captured Vanunu alongside a few supporters who were on the same SABEEL trip that I was on. As soon as I saw them I remembered that during that trip Vanunu told me, "I don't care about history. I don't owe history. All I want is to leave Israel and never return."

My third book covered Vanunu's life from childhood, through multiple crisis of faith, conscience and identity and documented his underreported historic freedom of speech trial in Israel through his release from 78 days back in solitary in the summer of 2010 because he spoke to foreign media in 2004. This book will document Vanunu's historic and underreported May 5, 2011 appeal to revoke his citizenship under Israel's Citizenship Revocation Law up through the last communication I have had from him as of November 24, 2012.

Three months after publishing BEYOND NUCLEAR: Mordechai Vanunu's FREEDOM of SPEECH Trial and My Life as a Muckraker: 2005-2010, I announced my candidacy as a Citizen of Conscience for US HOUSE 2012, District 5, Fl. on YouTube. That was when the crazy idea to run for congress morphed into a desire to serve in the House.

What I learned on the campaign trail is that I will never be a politician, but I will continue to write with hope to provoke change for the better in the political realm.

The Republicans held their presidential convention in Tampa, which is 'home' to the largest population of homeless people in Florida. The Republicans cancelled the first day of their convention due to fear of Hurricane Isaac, so The Media had nothing else to do but turn out for the counter demonstration on August 28, 2012.

The Media and Police far outnumbered the few hundred diverse citizens for justice, peace and equal human rights who joined The March on The RNC. We were blessed with cloud cover and a few short drizzles before the sun broke out on the hurricane of We The People who hold "these truths to be self-evident: That all [people] are created equal; that they are endowed by their creator with certain unalienable rights . . . that, to secure these rights, governments are instituted among [people] deriving their just powers from the consent of the governed; and, whenever any form of government becomes destructive of these ends, it is the RIGHT of the people to ALTER or to ABOLISH it."

The day before I reported from the Ron Paul Rally and captured guitar legend Jimmy Vaughn doing "DOWN WITH BIG BROTHER" for my YouTube Channel as I recalled George Orwell's nightmare titled "1984."

In it, Orwell relates the tale of Winston Smith, a solitary man with independent thought that Big Brother: The Party incarnate found so threatening that they tortured him beyond his endurance in order to break him, brainwash him and strip him of his humanity.

In the Centennial Edition of "1984", Thomas Pynchon wrote the Foreword and Erich Fromm the Afterword, from which I quote:

"A working prophet, is able to see deeper than most of us into the human soul. In 1948, Orwell understood that despite the Axis defeat, the will to fascism had not gone away . . . the irresistible human addiction to power was already long in place. The means of surveillance in Winston

Smith's era are primitive next to the wonders of computer technology: most notably the Internet."

"Universal peace and justice are the goals of man, and the prophets have faith that in spite of all errors and sins under the illusion of fighting for peace and democracy. All the fighting nations have lost moral considerations . . . the unlimited destruction of civilian populations and atomic bombs. Can human nature be changed so that man will forget his longing for freedom, dignity, integrity, love-can man forget that he is human?"

In Orwell's epic, Winston Smith played the role of the archetype of all threats to Big Brother; an individual with an open and free mind, independent thought, a memory of history and a voice of dissent who was willing to take bold action.

Orwell's Big Brother tortured all threats in order to get inside their head and then to brainwash them into accepting doublethink as truth.

I contend that today's Big Brother is an Industrial Media Congressional Military Security/Surveillance Complex, which as of this writing have not yet found the way to stop the free flow of info and independent thought streaming through the World Wide Web.

"Orwell demonstrates the illusion of the assumption that democracy can continue to exist in a world preparing for nuclear war. Leaders have only one aim, and that is power and power means to inflict unlimited pain and suffering to another human being. We spend a considerable part of our income and energy in building thermonuclear weapons, and close our minds to the fact that they might go off and destroy one third or one half of our population and that of the enemy. Another example of doublethink-from a Christian standpoint is the evil of killing any other. Can a minority of one be right?"

As a minority of one, I flew to Virginia in September to attend the 2012 LIBERTY Political Action Conference.

I was able to accomplish one of my missions when for the second time I personally handed the following questions to Congressman Ron Paul-via his body guard-the first time was to Ron Paul's Deputy Press Secretary, James V. Barcia, just prior to the WE ARE THE FUTURE RALLY at the University of South Florida's Sun Dome. But this time I also 'gifted' Dr. Paul with a copy of my third book, BEYOND NUCLEAR: Mordechai Vanunu's FREEDOM of SPEECH Trial and My Life as a Muckraker: 2005-2010 at a private reception for him during the 2012 LIBERTY Political Action Conference. My Questions:

Dear RON PAUL,

Will you support the grass roots initiative that is seeking to establish every June 8th as USS LIBERTY REMEMBRANCE DAY?

In April 1999, thirty-six members of the US House of Representatives signed a letter calling for Israel's Nuclear Whistle Blowers release from prison because they believed "we have a duty to stand up for men and women like Mordechai Vanunu who dare to articulate a brighter vision for humanity."

Were you one of the 36?

Thank you for any reply, Eileen Fleming
Founder of WeAreWideAwake.org
Candidate for US HOUSE, D. 5, Fl.

The evening before at a private meeting with Senators Mike Lee [R-UT], Jim DeMint [R-SC] and Rand Paul [R-KY] and witnessed by at least thirty others, I asked the three Senators if they would support establishing every June 8th as USS LIBERTY REMEMBRANCE DAY. Senator Lee maintained silence, Senator Paul gave me what I suppose was his 'politically correct' advice that I should not focus on old news and Senator DeMint admitted he was stumped and couldn't respond. As of this writing NOT ONE of those politicians has uttered a single public word about the USS LIBERTY or Israel's WMD, and thus my imagination fueled by conscience calls me to write all about it.

"Imagination means nothing without doing."
—Charlie Chaplin

One reason I ran for Congress is because I live in a very conservative area but I am liberal, "If by a liberal you mean someone who looks ahead and not behind, someone who welcomes new ideas without rigid reaction, someone who cares about the welfare of the people—their health, their housing, their schools, their jobs, their civil rights, and their civil liberties,—someone who believes we can break through the stalemate and suspicions that grip us in our policies abroad, if that is what you mean by a liberal, then I'm proud to say I'm a liberal."—John F. Kennedy

I also am a fiscal conservative, meaning I live within my means. I also believe that to whom much is given-much more is required and knowledge brings responsibility.

The ABC affiliate in Orlando, offered all the local 2012 candidates for federal office three minutes of television time. I used mine to say that if I were elected, I would write a House Resolution to end federal regulations on cannabis and allow the states the right to legalize [or not] and reap all the profits from cultivation to dissemination of cannabis.

i also said I would write a House Resolution to establish every June 8th as USS LIBERTY Remembrance Day because the LBJ Administration failed to support those troops that Israel attacked aboard America's premier spy ship as it navigated in international waters during The Six Day War, killed 34, wounded over 170 men and 45 years later these troops still call for justice.

I quoted George Washington's warning from his farewell address to, "Observe good faith and justice towards all nations; cultivate peace and harmony with all . . . and passionate attachments for others, should be excluded; and that, in place of them, just and amicable feelings towards all should be cultivated. The nation which indulges towards another a habitual hatred or a habitual fondness is in some degree a slave . . . a passionate attachment of one nation for another produces a variety of evils."

Today is Veterans Day, which originated on the first "Armistice Day" on Nov. 11, 1919, which marked the first anniversary of the end of World War I.

Congress passed a resolution in 1926 for an annual observance, and ever since 1938, Nov. 11 has been a national holiday.

In 1954, President Dwight D. Eisenhower signed legislation to change the name to Veterans Day as a way to honor all who served in American wars.

A year prior, Eisenhower admitted:

"Every gun that is made, every warship launched, every rocket fired signifies, in the final sense, a theft from those who hunger and are not fed, those who are cold and are not clothed. This world in arms is not spending money alone.

"It is spending the sweat of its laborers, the genius of its scientists, the hopes of its children.

"The cost of one modern heavy bomber is this: a modern brick school in more than 30 cities. It is two electric power plants, each serving a town of 60,000. It is two fine, fully equipped hospitals. It is some 50 miles of concrete highway.

"We pay for a single fighter plane with a half million bushels of wheat.

"We pay for a single destroyer with new homes that could have housed more than 8,000 people.

"This is not a way of life at all, in any true sense. Under the cloud of threatening war, it is humanity hanging from a cross of iron."

In his Farewell Address, Eisenhower warned of the potential for the "disastrous rise of misplaced power" from militarist interests that would gain control over this country's national security policy.

Any monkey can be trained to stand on a street and wave a flag, but only when we listen to our Veterans and act in their defense; do we truly Support The Troops!

June 8, 1967, remains a day in infamy that most Americans have no knowledge of, because The Media failed to pursue the story of Israel's wanton, unprovoked and brutal attack on the USS LIBERTY, America's premier spy ship, as it navigated in international waters off the coast of Egypt.

On October 13, 2007, I met my first LIBERTY survivor, then President of the USS LIBERTY Veterans Association, Petty Officer Phillip F. Tourney. We both spoke at the "No More Wars for Israel Conference" in Irvine, California. When Tourney said, "It was God that kept us afloat" I knew I would do more than just listen to him.

Tourney also said, "Thirty four Americans were brutally slaughtered, 172 wounded [including himself] when Israel deliberately attacked America's virtually unarmed LIBERTY in international waters, knowing full well our identity, in an assault that lasted as long as the attack on Pearl Harbor. The government of Israel put a knife in the back of America! The Israelis began the attack with unmarked jet fighters using rockets, canons, and napalm on our unprotected ship. Three motor torpedo boats fired six torpedoes at us, one hitting its mark—midship's on the starboard side, instantly blowing to bits 25 of America's finest young men.

"The American government colluded with Israel in the treasonous cover-up of the attack on the USS LIBERTY and the survivors were ordered to remain silent under threat of court martial, imprisonment or worse. The U.S. government has never challenged the obviously phony Israeli excuse of 'mistaken identity' nor have they attempted to expose the dishonorable cover up that continues to date. Truth and America's honor were ignominiously sacrificed to provide cover for Israel's transparent lies and despicable act of perfidy.

"Israel got away with cold blooded murder! Forty years ago the CIA and the NSA all threatened the survivors not to talk! They scared me so much I didn't for twenty years!

"Our keel was broken, we should have sunk but God kept us alive! Israel wanted the world to believe that Egypt [committed the crime]. Eighteen hours after the attack we were rescued and McNamara said, 'We're not going to attack our ally.' How did McNamara know who attacked us?"

On October 2, 2007, The Chicago TRIBUNE published a SPECIAL REPORT: THE STRIKE ON THE USS LIBERTY, from which I excerpt:

To a man, the survivors interviewed by the Tribune rejected Israel's explanation. Nor, the survivors said, did they understand why the American 6th Fleet, which included the aircraft carriers America and Saratoga, patrolling 400 miles west of the Liberty, launched and then recalled at least two squadrons of Navy fighter-bombers that might have arrived in time to prevent the torpedo attack—and save 26 American lives.

J.Q. "Tony" Hart, then a chief petty officer assigned to a U.S. Navy relay station in Morocco that handled communications between Washington and the 6th Fleet, remembered listening as Defense Secretary Robert McNamara, in Washington, ordered Rear Adm. Lawrence Geis, commander of the America's carrier battle group, to bring the jets home. When Geis protested that the Liberty was under attack and needed help, Hart said, McNamara retorted that "President [Lyndon] Johnson is not going to go to war or embarrass an American ally over a few sailors."

McNamara, who is now 91, told the Tribune he has "absolutely no recollection of what I did that day," except that "I have a memory that I didn't know at the time what was going on."

The Johnson administration did not publicly dispute Israel's claim that the attack had been nothing more than a disastrous mistake. But internal

White House documents obtained from the Lyndon B. Johnson Presidential Library show that the Israelis' explanation of how the mistake had occurred was not believed.

Except for McNamara, most senior administration officials from Secretary of State Dean Rusk on down privately agreed with Johnson's intelligence adviser, Clark Clifford, who was quoted in minutes of a National Security Council staff meeting as saying it was "inconceivable" that the attack had been a case of mistaken identity.

The attack "couldn't be anything else but deliberate," the NSA's director, Lt. Gen. Marshall Carter, later told Congress.

"I don't think you'll find many people at NSA who believe it was accidental," Benson Buffham, a former deputy NSA director, said in an interview.

"I just always assumed that the Israeli pilots knew what they were doing," said Harold Saunders, then a member of the National Security Council staff and later assistant secretary of state for Near Eastern and South Asian affairs.

"So for me, the question really is who issued the order to do that and why? That's the really interesting thing."—End John Crewdson, Tribune senior correspondent.

A few of the many interesting things about that day in infamy for me, were answered a week before Christmas 2007.

On June 8, 1967, Lieutenant Richard F. Kiepfer, was the lone medical doctor on board the spy ship, the USS LIBERTY, who "with complete disregard for his own personal safety, exposed himself to overwhelmingly accurate rocket and machine gun fire . . . administered first aid . . . treated [171 wounded] men for pain, shock . . . [and] conducted a major surgical operation" [Silver Star Medal Commendation].

Six weeks after boarding the LIBERTY, fifteen minutes into the attack and while operating on a sailor to control his bleeding, Dr. Kiepfer received

11

eleven shrapnel wounds into his abdomen, a gun shot to his leg, burns and a broken knee cap. He remained on his feet and caring for the crew for the next twenty-eight hours and their spirits ever since.

I visited with 70 year old Dr. Kiepfer, a Catholic born and bred in Brooklyn, in his Texas home where the deer ignore the corn put out by his neighbors, for Dr. Kiepfer provides prime feed in his front yard. Obese raccoons dine on a daily feast of dog food and multiple cats eat better than mine, in his back yard. Friends, who check on the doctor daily, set the food out, for Dr. Kiepfer could no longer do what he once did.

A Master Bridge player while still in his teens, Dr. Kiepfer today continues to play the cards he has been dealt in life with aplomb and grace. In 1973 he nearly died in a plane crash after parachuting atop of Georgia pecan trees that ended his surgical career and the use of his right hand and arm.

"As I laid there and looked at my arm and failed every test to move it, I knew then I would never operate again and began to think about what I could do in life to continue to be useful, and decided on nuclear medicine. The pilot landed a mile away from me, and was impaled on a forest of pine trees."

After twenty years in nuclear medicine he retired after suffering a heart attack and since then has suffered the loss of two wives, but not his sense of humor, which borders on the ribald. My weekend visit with Dr. Kiepfer in his home adorned with icons of St. Francis occurred only a week after his discharge from a rehabilitation center. He had spent the last six months recuperating from a below the knee amputation.

Retired Commander David Ed Lewis who had been the officer in charge of 195 men out of the total crew of 294 on the US LIBERTY, told me, "I know Doc has suffered more and complained less than anyone I know. Job didn't have much on Doc. He has always dedicated his life to others and has never asked anything in return from them."

The book of Job is a critique about the justice of God in light of suffering and finding meaning and value in that pain and not playing a blame game and I learned that Keipfer certainly qualifies. I also had many questions for Dr. Kiepfer, and utmost was what was left out of the Court of Inquiry: such as how could the deck log which documents the hours during the attack be so neatly written and list all the dead and wounded in alphabetical order within the hours of noon to four PM but make no mention of the many Israeli over flights that occurred during the morning before the attack?

Dr. Kiepfer explained, "The deck log was not written during the attack. Captain McGonagle signed off on the Log and that makes it legal, but not authentic. McGonagle was concerned that he would be blamed for the LIBERTY being in troubled waters. I told him, 'Over my dead fucking body!'"

After the hellacious and unprovoked attack by Israel, they did indeed blame the victims. "Israel did identify the ship six hours before the attack. Israel did know that the ship was American and admitted to our government that they knew the ship was American; Israel claims only that the attacking forces failed to get the word.

"Modern diplomacy simply does not permit one to embarrass a 'friendly' nation, even when that nation is caught red-handed with its torpedo in one's ship!

"McGonagle was tormented by the idea that he was somehow responsible for the agony his ship and crew suffered. One top level theory holds that someone in the Israeli armed forces ordered the LIBERTY sunk because he suspected that it had taken down messages showing that Israel started the fighting during the Six Day War.

"Typical of Israel's casual attitude toward the episode, an attitude which suggested from the beginning that it was really our fault for being there-in international waters-in the first place.

"Messages from Israel directly charged that a share of the blame was McGonagle's. The Shreveport Times suggested that our government was involved in a cover-up and that the attack itself may have been conducted to prevent the ship and the United States from detecting the pending invasion of Syria" which had been scheduled for June 8th but implemented on June 9th.

"McGonagle may have misremembered or may have not reported the over a dozen Israeli over flights that morning because he may have thought he should have abandoned our mission-which was to listen in on all communications. My opinion as a civilian is that the Court of Inquiry-which was to determine if the Navy were at fault—should have inquired why he didn't get the LIBERTY out of the area since we could see the smoke from Al Arish, in Gaza.

"I was the only Medical Corp officer to be appointed Officer of the Deck-that means I was in charge of everything on the ship when the Captain was off duty. I stood mid watch from midnight to 4 AM the night before the attack of June 8, 1967 and all was quiet. I always slept until 7:29 because breakfast ended at 7:30. Beginning at sunrise to 8 AM, the bridge reported a couple of propeller driven aircraft overhead and by noon several more. At lunch people were talking about all the Israeli over flights, but nobody was worried; they were our friends. Afterwards, as usual I went to the wardroom for coffee while the Corpsmen began the start of sick call and off duty officers pursued the national sport of sunbathing on the quarterdeck.

"Lieutenant George Golden and I were together when the attack began and we thought a steam line had ruptured when we heard the first explosion. We both headed off to our general quarters stations as the announcement sounded that we were under attack. I assumed it was perpetrated by the Arabs or Russians. Understand that nobody could identify Mirage fighter-bombers that travel at MACH One. IMAGINE as I say these words to you that the jets are a mile away, now they are overhead and now they are a mile away from us. That is how fast they travel.

"Fifteen minutes into the attack, while I was operating on a sailor and trying to control his bleeding, I was hit with eleven pieces of shrapnel into my abdomen. A rocket struck above the ceiling of sick bay and the light over my head and the operating table protected me; both acted as a life saver for me, otherwise I would have gotten hit in my shoulders, side and back. I was knocked against a wall and waves of red and white pain throbbed through me.

"I knew I had to finish with the guy on the table-if I walked away, I wouldn't have returned. All I could think about was keeping limbs attached to sailors. From the moment the attack began, I felt a greater presence within me that was physically holding me up. I thought it was the spirit of all the navy docs who had gone before me. I felt physically held up by my invisible assistants and with all that adrenalin coursing through me and some carefully titrated morphine that I self injected, I was able to do what I did.

"It was not until I finished that operation did I even examine myself. The fragments that penetrated me were so hot they cauterized my wounds. The pain was intense, but after applying surgical dressings to my wounds and putting on a life vest to control the bleeding I gave myself a shot of morphine and remained on my feet and working for the next twenty-eight hours.

"Just before the torpedo struck, I was summoned to the bridge and went through the mess decks from sickbay, where a number of wounded sailors were. Captain McGonagle was the only man still functioning there, the lookouts were dead, the helmsman-the guy at the steering wheel was dead and I saw the blown apart remains of our Navigator, Mr. Toth, two decks below me. All I could do was administer morphine to the still living and get them onto stretchers to evacuate them. I had two Corpsmen working with me and knew I needed more surrogates, for the wounded were shoulder to shoulder the full circumference of the passageway.

"While I was on the deck, I got hit by a fifty caliber machine gun bullet to my leg that came from the torpedo boats. I was bleeding into my shoes and not until the next day when i was able to lie down did the bleeding slow down. You know the story of the Incredible Hulk and mother's who lift cars off of their kids? When you are angry and hurt you can do amazing things.

"If you got one hundred people into my skin that day, probably all of them would have thrown up from the hell that erupted on the LIBERTY. Men were groaning and crying for their mothers, but it was just background noise for me. I was slip sliding as I crossed the bloody deck to get to the Captain who had been hit. McGonagle was leaning back in the Captain's chair, bleeding from many orifices; some natural and some new ones. I applied battle dressings, started an IV, gave him some morphine and sent an enlisted man to find as many officers as possible to come up to the Bridge and assist him and to watch him for shock. The Captain said, 'If I sit up, I pass out, but as long as I stay in this position, I am OK.'

"People I had eaten lunch with were dismembered all around me, burned, dead. To this day, every time I have a phone conversation with Phil Tourney, who held the light while I was operating on Blanchard, he tells me he can still see the look in my eyes.

"Everyone in the Navy hierarchy knew we were scapegoats and the Navy would have done anything to exact retribution, but the Navy never got the chance.

"In LBJ's mind we were just an average day's losses in Vietnam. I doubt Israel would have attacked without the knowledge or complicity of our State Departments willingness to sacrifice a few hundred sailors to have a 'stabilized' Middle East and all that oil. Our State Department's morality and ethics are just slightly below those of a Madame in a house of ill repute or a large-scale drug dealer.

"June 8, 1967 was like July 4th in hell without the ice cream. And yes, I agree that it was God that kept us afloat."

Ernest Gallo worked for the CIA for twenty-nine years after serving on the USS LIBERTY as a Second Class Petty Officer and Communications Technician. Ernie has also served as a President of the USS Liberty Veterans Association and is the founder of the Liberty Foundation. Ernie provided me with hard copies of written statements from LIBERTY survivors that I have not met along with his, and whom I have met.

On March 21, 2006, Gallo signed a notarized statement regarding how after the attack on the LIBERTY, he "went topside and viewed an Israeli helicopter with armed troops circling the ship. After a moment or two,

the helicopters flew away. The attack was now completely over . . . .
I witnessed unbelievable carnage. Pools of blood seemed to be in every
passageway . . . the dead and body parts helter-skelter . . ."

On Saturday, June 10, 1967 on stationary imprinted with "USS LIBERTY
AGTR-5" an Ensign named John wrote:

Dear Family, I AM ALIVE AND UNHURT. I cannot begin to tell you all that
has happened to us. It seems so unreal.

The entire crew was magnificent in their efforts to save the ship. We
were steaming unescorted about 15 miles off the Suez Canal-we were in
international waters!!

At about 2:00 PM we were first hit by jet fighters craft, which first
went for our guns—4 50cal. Machine guns. Every man save one on the
guns was killed in a matter of minutes. Next the aircraft hit the bridge
area. Wounded the C.O.-killed the executive officer and the navigator.
Everybody else was either wounded or killed on the bridge. Only three
men were left standing. Next they hit our antennas and our radio station.
All our boats and inflatable life rafts were hit—most destroyed. It was
a well-planned and coordinated attack. We had been shadowed by the
planes and PT boats all morning. Our FLAG was hoisted. I don't see how
they made a mistake. It was too well planned and coordinated—they
knew exactly where to hit us—and they did. Next we were attacked by 3
patrol crafts. One torpedo missed. The next one hit us forward starboard
side on the 3rd deck. It hit 20 feet from Damage Control Central-my
Battle station-it dislodged cabinets-threw books everywhere and knocked
us flat on the deck. A watertight bulkhead saved us [two phone talkers
and myself]. We patched up all holes in hull except torpedo hole-12'
by 15' and righted the ship. One more torpedo hit and we would have
gone down. The entire ship looks like hell. About a third of the crew is
wounded . . . 25 men were caught in the flooded spaces . . . never had
a chance to escape. We are heading for Malta . . . ###

Purple Heart recipient Warren D. Heaney, reported, "It took us 17 days
to limp to Malta. I had to go into the refrigerator over and over. The
food supplies were on my right and the body bags on my left. Thirty-four

dead and the smell throughout the ship was horrendous. We had no A/C working, so you can IMAGINE the results of blood and body parts everywhere in the June heat.

"I stayed aboard the LIBERTY the whole time we were in dry dock-34 days. I watched as the bodies were removed from the torpedo hole and put into body bags; all marked unidentifiable. A body after 17 days in water causes the skin to separate from the bones and muscles . . . Part of the horror of the whole thing is that we were sworn to secrecy, we were told not to speak to anyone about this, not even to each other.

"It wasn't until a LIBERTY veterans reunion, after talking to shipmates that I found out about PTSD. My shipmates told me how important it is for me to get help for my anger, anguish, and nightmares . . .

"I saw the faces of the men every day as they came through my chow line. Now they are dead and gone, but not forgotten. To this day the Unites States and Israel wish the LIBERTY veterans would just go away."

Radioman Glen Roger Oliphant recalled, "After the wounded were taken off the ship and the Sixth Fleet examined the ship, we proceeded towards Malta. For six nights we slept on the main deck for fear the ship might sink . . . . Admiral Kidd told the crew that we were not to discuss the attack with anyone and any communications to the press would be by the Navy. Every morning at muster in Malta the crew was told not to discuss the attack with anyone. The executive officer said we would be punished if we talked to anyone about the attack."

One of the memories Oliphant swore to unto perjury of law was after the order came to return to the transmitter room, he discovered there was no electricity to it and went on deck to discover the antennae base had a hole in it and observed three inflated life rafts floating behind the boat at a range of 100 to 150 yards. Then suddenly, tiny splashes appeared around the rafts and then deflated. Within minutes a torpedo boat appeared and stopped by the rafts. Someone picked up one of the rafts and put it in the torpedo boat. After several minutes the torpedo boat started up and approached the ship off the port side. I noticed a sailor manning a machine gun and he was pointing it right at me. I quickly lay down on the deck and crawled over to a chock hole and looked and he was still pointing the machine gun at me. I retreated and lay down for several minutes then I heard the torpedo boat start up and proceed along the port side. I looked at the torpedo boat when it was going by and observed a small flag with the Star of David on it and I knew it was an Israeli boat."

Maurice B. Shafer, wrote, "During our stay in Malta a board of inquiry was held and I had no part in this. I did have the experience of Admiral Kidd telling us to forget everything that happened. We were instructed that we could not talk about the attack and if we did we would be in major trouble. That was the beginning of the cover up in our eyes. The big part of the cover up was already under way in Washington."

In "The Untold Story of Israel's Deadly 1967 Assault on a U.S. Spy Ship" a son of a LIBERTY survivor, journalist and author James Scott blew apart the U.S. Naval Court of Inquiry, which confirmed Israel's claim of "mistaken identity".

Scott uncovered hundreds of interviews with LIBERTY survivors, senior administration and intelligence officials and accessed recently declassified documents by Israel and America.

Israeli pilots, air control staff and navy officers in Tel Aviv and Haifa were well aware that before their torpedo attacks on the unarmed spy ship that the vessel was definitely American. More than twenty minutes before the fatal torpedo strike that killed twenty-five sailors, Israel's chief air controller conclusively identified the LIBERTY as an American ship.

Many years after the attack, Lieutenant Colonel Shmuel Kislev, the chief air controller at general headquarters in Tel Aviv, confessed that he knew the U.S.S. LIBERTY was an American ship as soon as an Israeli pilot radioed in its hull numbers.

Two months before the sailor's mass burial at Arlington Cemetery, Navy analysis also uncovered that the Israeli torpedo boat gunners had targeted the spy ship with 40-mm tracer rounds made in the United States.

In 1967, the Republican representative from Iowa, H.R. Gross asked questions that still demand an answer today:

"Is this Government now, directly or indirectly, subsidizing Israel in the payment of full compensation for the lives that were destroyed, the suffering of the wounded, and the damage from this wanton attack? It can well be asked whether these Americans were the victims of bombs, machine gun bullets and torpedoes manufactured in the United States and dished out as military assistance under foreign aid."

By November 1967, lawmakers were willing to spend six million USA tax dollars to build schools in Israel but during the debate, Representative Gross spoke with the voice of conscience and introduced an amendment that "not one dollar of U.S. credit or aid of any kind [should] go to Israel until there is a firm settlement with regard to the attack and full reparations have been made [and Israel] provides full and complete reparations for the killing and wounding of more than 100 United States citizens in the wanton, unprovoked attack . . . I wonder how you would feel if you were the father of one of the boys who was killed in that connection-or perhaps you do not have any feelings with respect to these young men who were killed, wounded and maimed, or their families."

Gross's amendment failed, justice remains delayed and American tax payers continue to support the Ethnocratic State of Israel which has reaped a more violent and insecure planet.

In "An Israeli in Palestine: Resisting Dispossession, Redeeming Israel" Professor Jeff Halper, American Israeli and co-founder and coordinator of Israeli Committee Against House Demolitions explained:

"An ethnocracy is the opposite of a democracy, although it might incorporate some elements of democracy such as universal citizenship and elections. It arises when one particular group-the Jews in Israel, the Russians in Russia, the Protestants in pre-1972 Northern Ireland, the whites in apartheid South Africa, the Shi'ite Muslims in Iran, the Malay in Malaysia and, if they had their way, the white Christian fundamentalists in the US-seize control of the government and armed forces in order to enforce a regime of exclusive privilege over other groups in what is in fact a multi-ethnic or multi-religious society. Ethnocracy, or ethno-nationalism, privileges ethnos over demos, whereby one's ethnic affiliation, be it defined by race, descent, religion, language or national origin, takes precedence over citizenship in determining to whom a county actually 'belongs.'" [Page 74]

In the May 28, 1993, edition of <u>Yedioth Ahronoth</u>, Ariel Sharon explained:

"The terms 'democracy' or 'democratic' are totally absent from the Declaration of Independence. This is not an accident. The intention of Zionism was not to bring democracy, needless to say. It was solely motivated by the creation in Eretz-Isrel of a Jewish state belonging to all the Jewish people and to the Jewish people alone. This is why any Jew of the Diaspora has the right to immigrate to Israel and to become a citizen of Israel."

Since the October War in 1973, Washington has provided Israel with a level of support dwarfing the amounts provided to any other state. It has been the largest annual recipient of direct U.S. economic and military assistance since 1976 and the largest total recipient since World War ll. Israel receives about $3 billion in direct foreign assistance each year, which is roughly one-fifth of America's entire foreign aid budget. In per capita terms, the United States gives each Israeli a direct subsidy worth over $500 per year. This largesse is especially striking when one realizes that Israel is now a wealthy industrial state with a per capita income roughly equal to South Korea or Spain.

During fiscal year 2007, the Congressional Research Service's "U.S. Foreign Aid to Israel," written by Jeremy M. Sharp, Specialist in Middle Eastern Affairs, [updated January 2, 2008] reported that the US gave Israel at least $2,500.2 million in 2007. This number does not include the $137.894 million we spent on joint U.S.-Israeli missile defense projects or the $1.4 billion in loan guarantees made available to Israel in 2007.

While U.S. economic aid to Israel has been phased out, it has been replaced with increasing military aid paid for by American taxpayers with over $3.1 billion annually that go to provide even more weapons

21

of destruction to one of the most powerful militaries the world has ever known.

The United States has given more money to Israel than to any other country, and the indirect or consequential costs to the American taxpayer as a result of Washington's blind support for Israel exceed by many times the amount of direct U.S. aid to Israel. Some of these 'indirect or consequential' costs would include the costs to U.S. manufacturers of the Arab boycott, the costs to U.S. companies and consumers of the Arab oil embargo and consequent soaring oil prices as a result of U.S. support for Israel in the 1973 war, and the costs of U.S. unilateral economic sanctions on Iran, Iraq, Libya and Syria.

During the Bush Administration, Israel killed more than 3,000 Palestinian civilians-including more than 1,000 children during its December-January war on the Gaza Strip-with U.S. made weapons in violation of the Arms Export Control and Foreign Assistance Acts. In 2007, the United States Government agreed to increase military aid to Israel by 25% over the next decade, totaling $30 billion.

In May 2009, President Obama sent his FY2010 budget request to Congress, which included $2.775 billion in military aid for Israel, an increase of $225 million from the previous year's budget. That request came despite the fact that Israel consistently misuses U.S. weapons in violation of the Arms Export Control and Foreign Assistance Acts.

The Pentagon dismantled the spy ship program in 1968, but LIBERTY survivors and supporters continue to pursue justice. Israel paid minimal compensation to the families of the crew and six million for damages to the unarmed spy ship, which in fact should have exceeded 40 million. Israel has never acknowledged that the attack was premeditated and instead, blamed the victims.

George Ball was undersecretary of State under JFK and LBJ who not only called for an early end to America's War on Vietnam, he also believed our policy of underwriting all of Israel's actions in the Middle East was detrimental to America's interests. Ball's last book, "The Passionate Attachment: America's Involvement with Israel" notes:

"The LIBERTY'S presence and function were known to Israel's leaders. They presumably thought it vital that the LIBERTY be prevented from informing Washington of their intention to violate any cease-fire before they had completed their occupation of the Golan.

"The ultimate lesson of the LIBERTY attack had far more effect on policy in Israel than in America. Israel's leaders concluded that nothing they might do would offend the Americans to the point of reprisal. If America's leaders did not have the courage to punish Israel for the blatant murder of American citizens, it seemed clear that their American friends would let them get away with almost anything."

More recently, Admiral Moorer, General Raymond Davis, Rear Admiral Staring, Ambassador James Akins and others have come forth stating the attack was deliberate. They all asked for a new Court of Inquiry be convened by the Department of the Navy with Congressional oversight, to thoroughly investigate the attack on the USS LIBERTY, which is the only way justice can be rendered to the survivors.

Admiral Moorer and his distinguished colleagues also called for June 8th to be known as "USS LIBERTY Remembrance Day in order to commemorate the Liberty's heroic crew".

IF I had been elected to congress I would have written a House Resolution to establish every June 8th to be "USS LIBERTY Remembrance Day."

During my campaign I never met another candidate or elected official who said they would support that initiative, but I asked every one I met!

"If you want a vision of the future, IMAGINE a boot stomping on a human face-forever."—George Orwell

Today is November 14, 2012. I just returned home from moving my demented mother into a smaller apartment in an assisted living facility. Three weeks ago my father died from a massive stroke and heart attack, after five years of Alzheimer's, but I am grieving over Operation Pillar of Cloud, Israel's current air assault on the Gaza Strip. I recall what I read in November 2006, from Father Manuel, the parish priest at the Latin Church and School in Gaza:

"Gaza cannot sleep! The people are suffering unbelievably. They are hungry, thirsty, have no electricity or clean water. They are suffering constant bombardments and sonic booms from low flying aircraft. They need food: bread and water. Children and babies are hungry . . . people have no money to buy food. The price of food has doubled and tripled due to the situation. We cannot drink water from the ground here as it is salty and not hygienic. People must buy water to drink. They have no income, no opportunities to get food and water from outside and no opportunities to secure money inside of Gaza. They have no hope.

"Without electricity children are afraid. No light at night. No oil or candles . . . Thirsty children are crying, afraid and desperate. Many children have been violently thrown from their beds at night from the sonic booms. Many arms and legs have been broken. These planes fly low over Gaza and then reach the speed of sound. This shakes the ground and creates shock waves like an earthquake that causes people to be thrown from their bed. I, myself weigh 120 kilos and was almost thrown from

25

my bed due to the shock wave produced by a low flying jet that made a sonic boom.

"Gaza cannot sleep . . . the cries of hungry children, the sullen faces of broken men and women who are just sitting in their hungry emptiness with no light, no hope, no love. These actions are War Crimes!"

The buzz has also become louder regarding Israel using nuclear warheads on Iran's nuclear facilities claiming evidence that Tehran has hidden far more of its uranium enrichment capacity beneath a mountain than previously suspected.

Some say much of Iran's Fordow enrichment site near the city of Qom is now deep underground in a "zone of immunity" safe from conventional airstrikes. Defense Minister Ehud Barak coined the phrase "zone of immunity".

Another senior defense source said, "A decade ago when Ariel Sharon (the former prime minister who suffered a stroke in 2006) was in charge, it was relatively easy to strike Iran as its air defences were almost non-existent. Now they've upgraded and our tactics have to change."

Shaul Mofaz, head of the Kadima party and leader of the opposition is also a former defence minister and one of the few Israeli politicians privy to the country's nuclear secrets. He knows Prime Minister Benjamin Netanyahu is playing a dangerous game and he tried to warn Israelis during a press conference when he unveiled a poster showing a red mushroom cloud with the slogan: "Bibi will endanger Israel."

Netanyahu said he was prepared to strike Iran without the support of the US adding, "When David Ben-Gurion declared the foundation of the state of Israel, was it done with American approval?"

YES it was! President Truman also crossed out the words "Jewish state" on the draft of the Establishment of Israel that was sent to him and changed it to "State of Israel." Truman also agreed that the establishment of Israel's statehood was contingent upon Israel honoring the Universal Declaration of Human Rights. Two Articles Israel has flagrantly ignored include:

Article 13. (2) Everyone has the right to leave any country, including his own, and to return to his country.

Article 19.
Everyone has the right to freedom of opinion and expression; this right includes freedom to hold opinions without interference and to seek, receive and impart information and ideas through any media and regardless of frontiers.

And that leads me back to Israel's Nuclear Whistle Blower, Mordechai Vanunu, who has been denied the right to leave the state ever since he emerged from 18 years in a windowless tomb sized cell on April 21, 2004.

I met him first in June 2005. I saw him last in June 2009, and he told me:

"The Central Commander of the General Army testified in court that it is OK if I speak in public as long as I do not talk about nuclear weapons.

"I think the court will realize even if they send me back for three months-what will they do after that?

"It is all about freedom of speech and they cannot keep me here forever. They want revenge because I survived the system. The isolation in prison made me feel like I was loosing my mind. I felt like I was dying.

"Jesus Christ's strong message to the Israelis of 2,000 years ago is that they were wrong in rejecting him. By going to church I am reminding Israel of JC. JC and I both did a good job for humanity.

"Obama needs to wake up and talk and walk. But America has lost eight years. America needs to free itself from the Israeli state. Five million Jews should not dictate to America what they shall do.

"The USA needs to wake up from 9/11. That was when America lost her way."

Three months prior Vanunu wrote to the Nobel Peace Prize Committee:

Eileen Fleming

"I cannot be part of a list of laureates that include Simon Peres. Peres established and developed the atomic weapon program in Dimona in Israel . . . Peres was the man who ordered [my] kidnapping . . . he continues to oppose my freedom and release . . . WHAT I WANT IS FREEDOM AND ONLY FREEDOM . . . . FREEDOM AND ONLY FREEDOM I NEED NOW."

Peres was awarded the Nobel Peace Prize for playing a part in achieving the Oslo Declaration of Principles. Ever since, Peres has been most instrumental in helping to destroy the agreement.

"I'm sick and tired of hearing things from uptight short sided narrow minded hypocrites all I want is the truth, just give me some truth. I've had enough of reading things by neurotic psychotic pigheaded politicians all I want is the truth, just give me some truth . . . How do you sleep at night?"—John Lennon

On 18 September 2004, in London, Yoko Ono awarded Mordechai Vanunu a peace prize founded in memory of and in the spirit of John Lennon's "Give Me Some Truth" released in 1971.

Reuters quoted Ono that Vanunu was honored as a person who has "spoken out for the benefit of the human race by overcoming extreme personal difficulties and, in doing so, have allowed the truth to prevail. Hopefully [Vanunu] can come and receive the award himself. He did complete his sentence, it's not as though he's a criminal. The point is that it's another statement, a statement that the whole world can share and think about. People power is stronger than the power of institutions."

Seven years later, on May 5, 2011, Vanunu sent the following appeal to:

Mr. Eli Yishai Minister of Interior The State of Israel, Prime M Netanyahu, Foreign Minister Liberman, Defence Minister Barak, Justice Minister Neaman and President Peres:

I am Mordechai Vanunu that was kidnapped from Rome on September 30, 1986 by The Israeli Secret Services.

Vanunu's WAIT for Liberty

I was tried by The Jerusalem District Court and convicted of Aggravated Espionage, High Treason and Assisting the Enemy and I was sentenced to 18 years imprisonment. This followed an interview I gave to The London Sunday Times regarding the secret production of nuclear weapons materials in Israel.

I fulfilled the democratic principle of the right of the public to know.

I have served 18 years in Ashkelon Prison, mostly in solitary confinement.

I was released on 21 April 2004 with severe restrictions imposed by the Israeli Government.

Seven years past and the restrictions had been renewed again and again relying on The Emergency Laws from 1945.

Since my release I have lived 6 years in East Jerusalem and since September 2010 I live in Tel Aviv.

On June 1986 I was baptized to the Anglican Church.

Recently, (March 28, 2011), the Knesset passed a new law that revokes the citizenship of anyone who was convicted of espionage or treason.

25 years I am demanding and waiting to have my full freedom restored.

This law should be applied to my case and I am willing for my citizenship to be revoked and canceled.

I am writing to you today asking the state of Israel to cancel my citizenship.

This desire is not new and is not recent, but now it is supported by the new law to revoke citizenship.

I am asking and expecting the enforcement of this law to its letter and revoke my Israeli citizenship.

This law applies to me and I am ready for my citizenship to be canceled.

I don't have another citizenship but I would be able to get one easily during my forced stay here and for sure at the moment that I am allowed to leave.

In any case I here declare that my wish was and still is to cancel/revoke, in fact, my Israeli citizenship.

After all the 'treatment' that I have received from the State of Israel and its citizens, I do not feel, here, as a citizen or how a citizen should feel, I feel as an unwelcome citizen and treated as such by the state of Israel and its citizens.

Israeli media and in the streets of Israel, I am called and shouted at as a spy, 'The Atom Spy', and a traitor I am harassed and persecuted as the enemy of the state for 25 years.

I feel I am still imprisoned, still held as a hostage, by the state and its government.

After 25 years of ongoing, many and very hard punishments by the State of Israel, I wish the end to all punishments and my suffering, and wish the realization of the basic human right of freedom.

I would like to exercise my right to freedom of conscience, my right to choose not to be a citizen of Israel.

I have no interest in Israeli citizenship; I do not want to live here.

I ask you to cancel/revoke my citizenship here and now.

I ask you to let me be free from Israel as our dislike is mutual.

I HAVE NO SECRETS!

EVERYTHING I KNEW THEN, I HAVE PASSED ON TO THE ENGLISH PAPER IN 1986!!

IT IS TIME TO ALLOW ME TO LEAVE ISRAEL AFTER A QUARTER CENTURY OF IMPRISONMENT!—Mordechai Vanunu ###

Vanunu is still waiting for Israel to rule on that historic appeal. Vanunu was inspired to use Israel's Citizenship Revocation Law to his benefit as the law allows the courts to revoke the citizenship of anyone convicted of crimes against the state, such as treason which includes resisting the military occupation of Palestine.

Vanunu was convicted of treason, served 18 years in jail and began his 9th year of open-air captivity on April 21, 2012.

In the petition, Vanunu's lawyer Feldman said Vanunu is not able to "find his place in Israeli society" because he is hounded by the media and by the public, who still refer to him as the "nuclear spy".

Vanunu's many years of requesting to leave the country have been denied by Israel in the 'holy' name of SECURITY based on the grounds that he might reveal additional state secrets about a place he has not set foot into since 1985!

On October 10, 2011, Vanunu wrote, "even if they will cancel my citizenship, it doesn't mean they will send me free, they can still keep me here, but we believe this is the way out from Israel. If they will not cancel my Israel citizenship, then the court will decide to hear the case, and then the judges in the court hearing will decide if they will force the interior minister to follow his Israel laws, and cancel my citizenship. Any way they must let [me] go free after 25 years. VMJC."

On 18 March 2012, Vanunu wrote, "the way to prevent any war with Iran is by demanding, making many programs about Vanunu's Freedom now struggle, and publishing again all the interviews, Videos, and Dimona Photos. Telling Israel the first step in the Path for M.E. disarmament is let Vanunu go NOW!!"

Also in March, the Facebook Cause FREE Mordechai Vanunu, surpassed 5,000 members. As the Primary Administrator of that Cause, I issued a Global Call for supporters to do something to mark April 21st, which began the first day in the 9th year Vanunu has been waiting for his right to leave Israel.

I issued a PRWEB Press Release as Eileen Fleming for US House and held my event at Strawberry Fields, New York City. I was not surprised when The MEDIA was a No Show, but I wondered what could have happened if an event had happened in Israel.

But by June 2012, Israel had indicted freedom of the press! Israeli Attorney General Yehuda Weinstein announced the State would indict Haaretz journalist Uri Blau and charge him with unauthorized possession of classified documents.

Weinstein told reporters he would not accuse the journalist of traditional espionage in this case that involved classified documents that Blau received from then-IDF soldier Anat Kam, who is currently serving a prison term of 4.5 years for passing on classified information.

The Israel SECURITY Agency/Shin Bet/Shabak, the State Prosecutor's Office, and the Israel Police all sought the indictment.

In his statement, Weinstein claimed, "Blau blatantly broke the agreement he signed, allegedly lied to investigators and handed over only a small part of the stolen military information he received. The potential for damage in the unprotected possession of the documents was enormous."

Blau had recently returned to Israel in accordance with the agreement made with the Prosecutor's Office and he maintains he turned over all the documents he received from Kam and others sources. Blau also agreed to undergo a lie detector test.

The State Prosecutor's office stated it will indict Blau, because he "betrayed his duty—and later his commitment before the state—to cease possession of them."

The Israeli Justice Department said the decision was made "after taking into account all of the relevant considerations, including the need to restrain the enforcement policy in order to maintain the Israeli press as a free press which fulfills its duty."

The duty of The Press is to seek and report the truth!

"All material published in Hebrew in Israel must be checked by military censors prior to publication and the military regularly obtains gag orders from the court system to prevent reporting of events, such as the Anat Kam affair."

Senior Yedioth Ahronoth [where Kam had worked] journalist Yigal Serena stated that Weinstein's decision "is part of the attempts to silence journalists in Israel. The problem isn't that reporters have access to confidential materials. There is a long, ongoing decline in investigative journalism in Israel and this is another step in it. This didn't come up out of nowhere. This is part of the long process of the collapse of free press. The AG just put another nail in the coffin."

Kam's conviction was Israel's second highest profile case of whistle blowing followed by imprisonment, second only to Israel's Nuclear Whistle Blower, Mordechai Vanunu.

Up until October 1985, Vanunu worked as a low-to-mid-level technician at the Dimona Nuclear Facility. In September 1986, he was kidnapped by the Mossad for telling the truth and providing the photographic proof to the London Sunday Times, which published a front page story confirming the existence of Israel's much denied plutonium separation plant.

When Vanunu last set foot into Israel's WMD facility in 1985, the plant was buried eighty feet below ground in the Negev desert. Ever since the 1960's, the Dimona has been used to recover plutonium from spent fuel rods.

Vanunu's real 'crime' was speaking the truth. And for that he was made to suffer a fate worse than death, nearly all of his eighteen years behind bars were in solitary confinement. Isolation is a well-known form of torture that can cause deep emotional scars and mental impairment. During this period Vanunu was also subjected to constant harassments and humiliations orchestrated by the Mossad to break his will and drive him crazy. Amnesty International described the conditions of Vanunu's ordeal as "cruel, inhuman, and degrading."

One of the causes for which Vanunu risked his life for was briefly realized in February 1999, when a debate of the nuclear issue exploded on the floor of the Israeli Knesset. The event was short-lived. After shouting and recriminations, several Arab members of the Knesset who had sparked the debate were expelled from the chamber.

Also in 1999, thirty-six members of the House of Representatives signed a letter calling for Vanunu's release from prison because they believed "we have a duty to stand up for men and women like Mordechai Vanunu who dare to articulate a brighter vision for humanity."

President Clinton responded with a public statement expressing concern for Vanunu and the need for Israel and other non-parties to the Non-Proliferation Treaty to adhere to it and accept IAEA safeguards, but ever since the silence from the American Government has been deafening!

On 24 April 2004, Uri Avnery, founder of the Gush Shalom peace movement as well as a member of the Irgun as a teenager and member of the Knesset for 11 years wrote:

"Everybody understands that Vanunu has no more secrets. What can a technician know after 18 years in jail, during which technology has advanced with giant steps?

"But gradually it becomes clear what the security establishment is really afraid of. Vanunu is in a position to expose the close partnership with the United States in the development of Israel's nuclear armaments.

"This worries Washington so much, that the man responsible in the State Department for 'arms control', Under-Secretary John Bolton, has come to Israel in person for the occasion. Vanunu, it appears, can cause severe damage to the mighty super-power.

"The Americans, it seems, are very worried. The Israeli security services have to dance to their tune. The world must be prevented by all available means from hearing, from the lips of a credible witness, that the Americans are full partners in Israel's nuclear arms program, while pretending to be the world's sheriff for the prevention of nuclear proliferation."

Also in 2004, Haaretz reporter, Yossi Melman wrote:

"This is the secret that hasn't yet been told in the affair: the story of the security fiasco that made it possible for Vanunu to do what he did, and the story of the subsequent attempts at cover-up, whitewashing and protection of senior figures in the defense establishment, who were bent on divesting themselves of responsibility for the failure. The 18-year prison term to which Vanunu was sentenced is almost exactly the same period as that in which Yehiel Horev has served as chief of internal security in the defense establishment [who has been] involved in the affair as deputy chief of security at the Defense Ministry, and also after Vanunu's abduction and arrest, as a member of an investigative commission.

"Shortly after taking office as chief of security at the Defense Ministry, Horev began to take punitive measures to hobble Vanunu. He is responsible for the harsh conditions in which Vanunu was held, which included years in solitary confinement, and the sharp limitations on the number of visitors he could have . . . [and has fought] a rearguard battle to prevent Vanunu from leaving Israel and to place him under supervision and restrictions that will be tantamount to house arrest. Horev has always been considered the strictest of all the security chiefs in Israel, especially in regard to the protection of institutions such as the Dimona facility and the Biological Institute. He is apprehensive that if Vanunu goes abroad, he will continue to be a nuisance by stimulating the public debate over Israel's nuclear policy and the nuclear weapons he says Israel possesses . . . all the hyperactivity being displayed by Horev and those who support his approach is intended only to divert attention from what has not yet been revealed: the security blunders and their cover-ups."

Vanunu has come to symbolize the intractable problem of state secrecy that stymies all efforts toward world nuclear disarmament and the US press ignores Vanunu's saga, which when well known will serve as an embarrassment to them as well as Israel and the US government.

Cases in point: In October 2011, the Tel Aviv District Court sentenced former Israel Defense Forces soldier Anat Kam to four-and-a-half years in prison for "collecting, holding and passing on classified information without authorization".

Kam was convicted in February 2012, under a plea bargain admitting guilt to gathering and storing of over 2,000 classified military documents from the Central Command office [under Maj. Gen. Naveh] during her army service.

Kam passed on the documents to reporter Uri Blau whose investigative report in Haaretz Magazine exposed misconduct by the Israel Defense Forces/IDF.

"The report reveals that the IDF had approved well in advance the targeted killing of Malaisha [on June 20, 2007, during a routine military raid in the West Bank] contravening the High Court ruling and intentionally misleading the public. The report was attributed to 'classified IDF documents' and had been approved by the Military Censor before going to press."

Blau made use "of classified material from those documents as the basis for two newspaper articles. In the first, published in late October 2008, Blau accused the IDF of defying a High Court of Justice ruling against the targeted killings of Palestinian terrorists. The next article, published a few weeks later, similarly intimated that the IDF had earmarked Palestinian terrorists for targeted killings, and included a photocopy of a targeted-killing order Kam had given Blau."

In her own testimony, Kam described "Maj. Gen. Naveh's office as 'embarrassing in terms of information security' and testified that she had not undergone any security check prior to being assigned to her army role, even though she had access to the most confidential documents."

Vanunu's WAIT for Liberty

Vanunu embarrassed Israeli SECURITY when he managed to photograph top-secret locations inside the Dimona because a supervisor carelessly left the keys to the restricted areas in the shower room.

Twenty-four years after the Mossad kidnapped Vanunu from Rome after luring him from London, they returned to track down another who followed his conscience but was labeled a traitor by a state who view truth tellers as a threat to their sense of security.

The prey that time was Uri Blau, who went into hiding after writing a series of reports exposing lawbreaking approved by Israeli army commanders.

Blau went underground to escape a potential lengthy jail term for espionage, for Israeli security services warned they would "remove the gloves" and track down the "fugitive felon."

The military censor, who prevents publication of information that they deem could harm Israel's national security, approved Blau's story for publication in Haaretz.

Kam had originally been charged under Israel's espionage and treason laws but the amended indictment dropped the charge of deliberately intending to harm state security, which carries a maximum penalty of life imprisonment.

The Israeli court initially gagged all news and details of Kam's arrest but after a cyber storm of Internet reporting, the gag order was lifted.

Shortly after her arrest, Kam admitted to copying the documents while serving in the office in charge of operations in the West Bank, between 2005 and 2007.

Then 23 years old, Kam said she acted out of conscience to expose war crimes and she believed she would be forgiven for her honesty and integrity.

A prelude to the Kam affair began in July 2009, when Kam's brothers in spirit from Breaking the Silence, an Israeli human rights group published 54 testimonies from Israeli soldiers regarding their experiences during Operation Cast Lead.

The testimonies exposed the gaps between the reports given by the army in January 2009 regarding the "accepted practices; the destruction of hundreds of houses and mosques for no military purpose, the firing of phosphorous gas in the direction of populated areas, the killing of innocent victims with small arms, the destruction of private property, and most of all, a permissive atmosphere in the command structure that enabled soldiers to act without moral restrictions."

On February 3, 2010, The Independent reported that a high-ranking officer who served as a commander during Operation Cast Lead, admitted that Israel's army went beyond its previous rules of engagement on the protection of civilian lives and "that he did not regard the longstanding principle of military conduct known as 'means and intentions'—whereby a targeted suspect must have a weapon and show signs of intending to use it before being fired upon—as being applicable before calling in fire from drones and helicopters in Gaza last winter."

On November 8, 2012, following a two-week period of quiet, Israel invaded Gaza. During an exchange of gunfire, Israeli troops shot 13-year-old Ahmed Younis Khader Abu Daqqa in the abdomen while he was playing soccer. Ahmed died later from his wounds. A Palestinian rocket killed 3 Israeli civilians.

On November 12, 2012, Palestinian militant groups agreed to a truce if Israel ceased military operations. Israel responded to this offer by engaging in an extrajudicial assassination of Hamas leader Ahmed Jabari on November 14. An Israeli peace activist was negotiating with Jabari a permanent truce between Israel and Palestinian militant groups when he was assassinated.

On November 18, 2012, an Israeli airstrike on the residential neighborhood of Naser in Gaza City killed at least 12 people, including at least 10 members of the Al-Dalu family, many of who were children and women.

Yesterday was World Children's Day. Tomorrow is Thanksgiving Day. Today I learned that Israel's military offensive on Gaza has now killed over 140 Palestinians, 32 of whom are children. Already over 1,100 Palestinians with 40% being children, have been injured as a result of the weeklong campaign.

Secretary General of the Palestinian National Initiative, Dr. Mustafa Barghouti, stated that there is no safe place in the Gaza Strip, "I am completely horrified by the scenes I witnessed in Gaza City's Shafa Hospital. This is not a war; this is a massacre. I have been a medical doctor for over 33 years. I have witnessed countless wars and atrocities but I have never before seen this level of brutality. We believe they [the Israeli military] have been using depleted uranium shells."

Barghouti also expressed condemnation of Israel's unchecked aggression against journalists. The number of journalists killed and wounded clearly illustrate that the Israeli military are targeting those who are trying to uncover and expose the truth to the rest of the world.

Israel's attacks against the Gaza Strip are being committed with U.S. weapons given to Israel as military aid by the U.S. taxpayer. These weapons are being misused by Israel in violation of the U.S. Arms Export Control Act to commit grave human rights abuses of Palestinians.

All people living under military occupation have the right of self-defense. International law forbids the targeting of civilians in hostilities. Israel employs disproportionate force to injure and kill civilians and destroy Palestinian infrastructure, which is not self-defense, but a furtherance of its illegal blockade and siege of the Gaza Strip.

The United States provides weapons to Israel at U.S. taxpayer expense. The United States also funds Israel's Iron Dome anti-missile system. By providing Israel the weapons to both attack Palestinians and shoot down Palestinian rocket fire, the United States has made it virtually cost-free financially for Israel to escalate its attacks on Palestinians.

And both the House and the Senate passed identical resolutions by a unanimous vote, that affirmed each chambers "strongly support" of

Israel's "inherent right to act in self-defense to protect its citizens against acts of terrorism."

The only violence the resolution condemned was the violence from Hamas. Not a word about State Terrorism, not a word about Israel's assassination of Hamas's military leader, not a word about Israel's illegal blockade of Gaza, not a word about the suffering of Palestinians under a Military Occupation aided and abetted by American policy and USA Taxpayers hard earned dollars.

If I had been elected to congress, I IMAGINE I would have immediately called for a cease-fire and I would have initiated an investigation into Israel's misuse of U.S. weapons in violation of U.S. law that injured and killed Palestinian civilians and journalists.

"Imagination is more important than knowledge. Knowledge is limited. Imagination encircles the world."
—Albert Einstein

On May 2, 2012, Israeli press reported that the Military Censor announced that the Israeli Defense Forces launched a new system to monitor information on Facebook, Twitter, blogs and news sites.

On April 22, 2012, I TWEETED to Vanunu, 60Minutes, President Peres, Netanyahu, Whitehouse and IsraelinUSA: "SECURITY ALERT RE: Israel's WMD and VANUNU" with a link that led to the book page on my website that leads with this quote from Abraham Lincoln: "I am a firm believer in the people. If given the truth, they can be depended upon to meet any national crisis. The great point is to bring them the real facts."

Not one replied, but I feel my message got through to Power for Vanunu disappeared from TWITTER a few hours after I received his private message via Facebook on May 1, 2012:

"Hi. Today they sent first notice, they will renew the restrictions, sent to my Lawyer. Now you are free, we can close the Cause. Either you do it or I will do it. I am going to deactivate my Facebook, very soon.

A few hours later, Vanunu's icon at the Facebook Cause "FREE MORDECHAI VANUNU" become a ghost. A few days later I resumed my previous position as lone administrator until I was able to secure some help. I deactivated my Facebook Wall on November 6th, and by then the Cause had grown to 6,452 members.

I IMAGINE the best that can be hoped for is that every member acts as a gnat in the eye, a mosquito on the neck or a royal pain in the ass to all who want the world to forget that all Vanunu did twenty-six years ago was tell the truth and provide the photographic proof that led nuclear physicist, Frank Barnaby to testify at Vanunu's closed door trial:

"I found Vanunu very straightforward about his motives for violating Israel's secrecy laws he explained to me that he believed that both the Israeli and the world public had the right to know about the information he passed on. He seemed to me to be acting ideologically.

"Israel's political leaders have, he said, consistently lied about Israel's nuclear-weapons programme and he found this unacceptable in a democracy. The knowledge that Vanunu had about Israel's nuclear weapons, about the operations at Dimona, and about security at Dimona could not be of any use to anyone today. He left Dimona in October 1985."

A total of 1,200 pages of transcript of that closed-door trial have been released. Vanunu told the court: "I wanted to confirm what everyone knew, I didn't want Israel to go on denying that it had nuclear weapons, and Shimon Peres to go on lying to (then US president) Ronald Reagan, saying that we didn't have a nuclear arsenal. I also wanted controls to be placed on these weapons. When I decided to expose Israel's nuclear weapons I acted out of conscience and to warn the world to prevent a nuclear holocaust."

Now, as Vanunu had sent out less than thirty TWEETS to less than thirty followers, the very fact that he disappeared from TWITTER and Facebook leaves no doubt in my mind that he remains under pressure from SECURITY/Mossad/Shabbak and their many helpers known as Sayanim, who also monitor this reporter.

By now 'they' must realize that WHY I do, what I do and WHY I won't and can't shut up is because I "Write about what disturbs me, particularly as it bothers no one else" [a paraphrase of a line in "The HELP" by Kathryn Stockett].

That is exactly what I have been doing since THAT DAY we call 9/11; and even more so after a serendipitous meeting with Vanunu on the first day of summer in 2005. I was most interested in his crisis of faith and culture, which began when his family resettled in Beersheba in 1963 when he was nine. Being nine months older than Vanunu, as he recalled those memories I remembered that at the same time America was grieving the unimaginable, incomprehensible loss of President Kennedy.

It was during those initial interviews that I also began to imagine Vanunu suffering an ongoing crucifixion just because twenty-six years ago, he told The TRUTH about Israel's nukes just a few weeks after becoming a Christian-the 'unpardonable sin' for particular Jews.

A few weeks before being kidnapped by the Mossad in September 1986, Vanunu was baptized at a social justice Episcopal Church in Sydney, Australia. Within minutes of emerging from his windowless tomb sized cell on April 21, 2004, Vanunu announced, "I am not harming Israel. I am not interested in Israel. I want to tell you something very important. I suffered here 18 years because I am a Christian, because I was baptized into Christianity. If I was a Jew I wouldn't have all this suffering here in isolation for 18 years. Only because I was a Christian man."

Vanunu was placed under draconian restrictions including not to speak to foreigners and not to leave the country. He gave hundreds of interviews in 2004 and on April 30, 2007, the Jerusalem Magistrate's Court, convicted Vanunu on 14 [out of 21] counts of violating a court order prohibiting him from speaking to foreign journalists in 2004.

Vanunu was also convicted for traveling from Jerusalem to Bethlehem to attend Christmas Eve mass at the Church of the Nativity, his first Christmas after being released from 18 years in jail. He spent that night behind prison bars instead.

On July 2, 2007, Israel sentenced Vanunu to six months in jail for speaking to foreign media in 2004 [it was reduced to 78 days in solitary in the summer of 2010.]

Two days before President Bush's first trip to Israel and a day before Vanunu's appeal was to begin, Israel sentenced him to community service instead.

On Feb. 5, 2008, Vanunu met with prison officials to arrange community service and learned that to his "surprise they say there is no community service in East Jerusalem. I told them the agreement for community service was on this condition that it will be only in the East Jerusalem. They say no one told them about this . . . I will do community service in the East Jerusalem or the appeal begins and may be the prison sentence."

On September 23, 2008, the Jerusalem District Court reduced Vanunu's sentence to three months, "In light of (Vanunu's) ailing health and the absence of claims that his actions put the country's security in jeopardy."

In November 2009, Vanunu suffered another crisis of faith and "fired God" from his case.

He emailed me the long version of his spin on 1 Corinthians 13, but also went public on his You Tube Channel:

"1 FREEDOM 13:1-13 If I speak in the tongues of men and angels, but have not FREEDOM, I have become sounding brass or a tinkling symbol. And if I have prophecy and know all mysteries and all knowledge, and if I have all faith so as to remove mountains, but have not FREEDOM, I am nothing. And if I know all mysteries and all knowledge, and speak in the tongues of men and angels, BUT HAVE NO FREEDOM, I am NOTHING. And if I have all faith so as to remove mountains, but have not FREEDOM, I am NOTHING."

On May 23, 2010, Israel sent Vanunu back to solitary confinement in a maximum prison facility and released him on August 8, 2010.

Vanunu emerged in a blazing red shirt and immediately became active on the World Wide Web at his You Tube Channel, and within a short time made nearly 1,000 Facebook Friends. But Vanunu soon whittled them down to 46 and finally deactivated his account on May 6, 2012.

Among the last few communications I have had from Vanunu since include:

July 10, 2012: Hi. You can continue to act and do for my freedom as much as you can-no one can stop you. Freedom NOW!!! vmjc.

July 11, 2012: The restrictions now renewed for the 9th year. My Lawyer Avigdor Feldman is trying to deal with the Israel authorities to find any solution to end this case, either by appeal to the court or by meeting with them. If you want to know more you can contact him, VMJC.

I did email Vanunu's attorney a few times, but no reply came and Vanunu warned me not to expect one.

On November 19, 2012, I wrote to Vanunu via YouTube: "18 months since your appeal and still Vanunu WAITS for freedom. 18 years in jail for telling THE TRUTH and into the 9th under virtual house arrest. What does SECURITY want to end their vendetta against VMJC?

On November 20, 2012, Vanunu re-uploaded his silent scrolling petition of May 5, 2011, but this time accompanied by an electronic disembodied voice and I IMAGINE Vanunu may be just as silenced by SECURITY as he was in 1986 on his way to his closed-door trial:

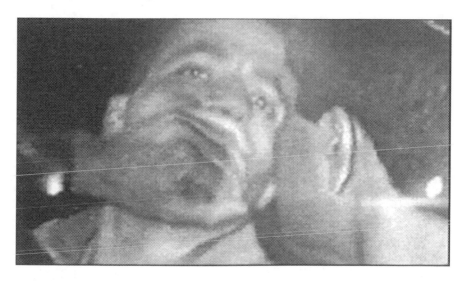

When I email Vanunu, the SUBJECT usually reads: SECURITY ALERT because the restrictions that have subjected him to 24/7 surveillance—his movements, phone calls and emails-by Israel's SECURITY spies-Mossad/Shabak ever since he emerged from 18 years in a windowless tomb sized cell on 21 April 2004 come from the Emergency Defense Regulations, which were implemented by Britain against Palestinians and Jews after World War II.

Attorney Yaccov Shapiro, who later became Israel's Minister Of Justice, described the Emergency Defense Regulations as "unparalleled in any civilized country: there were no such laws in Nazi Germany."

Just a few weeks after Vanunu's FREEDOM of SPEECH Trial began, and during my March 2006 visit to Israel Palestine, I began the taping of "30 MINUTES With Vanunu" by asking him, "If the British Mandate has expired why not the British Mandate's Emergency Defense Regulations?"

Vaunu replied, "The reason given is SECURITY but it is because Israel is not a democracy unless you are a Jew. This administration tells me I am not allowed to speak to foreigners, the Media, and the world. But I do because that is how I prove my true humanity to the world. My freedom of speech trial began January 25, 2006 for speaking to the media, the same day as the Palestinian elections."

"You cannot talk like sane men around a peace table while the atomic bomb itself is ticking beneath it. Do not treat the atomic bomb as a weapon of offense; do not treat it as an instrument of the police. Treat the bomb for what it is: the visible insanity of a civilization that has ceased . . . to obey the laws of life."—Lewis Mumford, 1946

Mordechai Vanunu, April 16, 2012

Mordechai Vanunu at St. Stephens Church, East Jerusalem.
Copyright Meir Vanunu, November 2007

Vanunu at the American Colony, east Jerusalem, June 14, 2009.

The icon most people knew me by at Facebook

Eileen Fleming at The Wall in Bethlehem.
Copyright Meir Vanunu, Nov. 2007

My view of The Wall from a rooftop in Bethlehem

When I told Helen Thomas I wanted to do The Colbert
Report, she responded, "That's toxic!" But agreed to
humor me doing my best Stephen impression.

Daffodil/Narkis P. Alfi, freelance correspondent and Likud Party
member with Eileen Fleming at AIPAC's 2011 conference.

An announcement of my run for US HOUSE and the
book cover of my third book flashed during a few rush
hours in Times Square, New York City, May 2012.

"Reality leaves a lot to the IMAGINATION."—John Lennon

In 2011, when I heard the call to "Move Over AIPAC: Building a New US Middle East Policy" I immediately became one of over 100 organizations to endorse it. I didn't commit to attend the event until I learned that journalist Helen Thomas was to be the keynote speaker.

By the time I booked my flight, Ms. Thomas had been "disinvited" because of the pressure from a few particular people who had still not gotten over her flaming honesty expressed on May 27, 2010, in a courtyard at the White House. As "life is what happens while you are making other plans" [John Lennon] their shortsightedness led to one of the highlights of my life.

My evening with Ms. Thomas was made possible by my friend Rich Forer, the author of "Breakthrough: Transforming Fear Into Compassion—A New Perspective on the Israel-Palestine Conflict."

After reading it, Ms. Thomas wrote, "People need to be informed so we can make good decisions regarding our involvement in the Middle East, and ultimately support the right governments. Forer offers a viewpoint that is not available in the mainstream. I admire Forer's courage to not being silent. He openly shares his personal transformation, and encourages the reader to be willing to 'assess one's beliefs with honesty and to follow wherever the facts lead'. The truth cannot be silenced."

During Jewish Heritage Month in 2010, in a courtyard at the White House, blogger and Long Island Rabbi David Nesenoff approached Ms. Thomas and introduced her to two young boys with him who were interested in a career in journalism.

Nesenoff asked, "So what do you think of Israel? Got any advice? Go for it" as he pointed his camera at Ms. Thomas like a "jackknife" and she readily replied, "They should get the hell out of Palestine."

In an interview with Playboy, Ms. Thomas elaborated, "I knew I'd hit the third rail. You cannot say anything about Israel in this country. But I've lived with this cause for many years. Everybody knows my feelings that the Palestinians have been shortchanged in every way. Sure, the Israelis have a right to exist—but where they were born, not to come and take someone else's home. I've had it up to here with the violations against the Palestinians. Why shouldn't I say it?"

Ms. Thomas's truth telling troubles in the USA may only have been surpassed by John Lennon, who in 1966, commented to a friend and reporter that the Beatles were more popular with my generation than Jesus was. Lennon endured a firestorm of media attacks, but none inquired as to WHY did kids like me who went to mass every Sunday and catechism every Wednesday afternoon, never quote Jesus but knew every lyric to every Beatles song.

Ms. Thomas was relentlessly attacked in the media and although she issued an apology, she abruptly "retired" meaning forced to retire from Hearst Newspapers on June 7, 2010. Her speaking agency dropped her, journalism schools and organizations rescinded awards named in her honor and she lost her front row seat in the White House pressroom; all because she audaciously spoke her heart and mind.

And all she was talking about is how Israel denies Palestinians the right to return to their homeland, but any Jew without any historical connection to the so-called Holy Land is encouraged by the state of Israel to colonize upon legally owned Palestinian property.

An Israeli citizen and volunteer with Israeli Committee Against House Demolitions in Jerusalem, told me, "There is an advertisement that runs in the USA that reads: 'Have a Holiday Home in Jerusalem.' The ad does not mention this home is 100% ILLEGAL! There are forty-two illegal settlements in the Muslim, Christian and Armenian quarters of Jerusalem. The only green area for [Palestinian] children to play will soon have a high rise for the settlers, which will be 7 meters taller than the walls of the Old City! The Wall has been deemed illegal by the International Court of Justice [in 2005] but America continues to allow it to grow. The wall is way over the Green Line proving it is not about security but about grabbing Palestinian land. Israel's policy of Quiet Transfer: getting rid of the Palestinians is a huge humanitarian crisis. It is clear how the wall zig zags that it is not about security but about grabbing the maximum land with minimal Palestinian occupation."

During my evening with Ms. Thomas I also filled her in on my distress over Amy Goodman's failure to follow up on her 2004 interview. In April 2007, I had lunch with Amy Goodman and filled Amy in on the fact that her one and only interview with Vanunu was major testimony against him in his FREEDOM of SPEECH trial. I asked her to please follow up before his sentence came down and she acted interested and jotted down notes in her Blackberry. But Amy didn't bother to call Vanunu until July 2007 after he was sentenced to 6 more months in jail essentially for speaking to her in 2004! When I saw Vanunu a few weeks later he told me he refused to speak to Amy again because she—like all THE MEDIA-hadn't done anything to help him raise awareness about Israel's continuing persecution of him.

In reply to my outpouring, Ms. Thomas replied, "She used to be better."

I then brought up Ms. Thomas's first and final question to President Obama regarding Middle East nuclear weapons, which he blew off claiming he didn't want to "speculate." The Media remained mute, and some even rolled their eyes and smirked when Thomas countered, but Obama moved on and The Media missed another opportunity to address the reams of documentation our State Department has on file regarding Israel's WMD.

Ms. Thomas replied, "They have no conscience."

I also claim their lack of integrity borders on treason!

I was not a reporter when I met Vanunu for the first time in June 2005, but I knew I had to become one when he told me:

"Did you know that President Kennedy tried to stop Israel from building atomic weapons? In 1963, he forced Prime Minister Ben Guirion to admit the Dimona was not a textile plant, as the sign outside proclaimed, but a nuclear plant. The Prime Minister said, 'The nuclear reactor is only for peace.'

"Kennedy insisted on an open internal inspection. He wrote letters demanding that Ben Guirion open up the Dimona for inspection.

"The French were responsible for the actual building of the Dimona. The Germans gave the money; they were feeling guilty for the Holocaust, and tried to pay their way out. Everything inside was written in French, when I was there, almost twenty years ago. Back then, the Dimona descended seven floors underground.

"In 1955, Perez and Guirion met with the French to agree they would get a nuclear reactor if they fought against Egypt to control the Sinai and Suez Canal. That was the war of 1956. Eisenhower demanded that Israel leave the Sinai, but the reactor plant deal continued on.

"When Johnson became president, he made an agreement with Israel that two senators would come every year to inspect. Before the senators would visit, the Israelis would build a wall to block the underground elevators and stairways. From 1963 to '69, the senators came, but they never knew about the wall that hid the rest of the Dimona from them.

"Nixon stopped the inspections and agreed to ignore the situation. As a result, Israel increased production. In 1986, there were over two hundred bombs. Today, they may have enough plutonium for ten bombs a year."

After cheesecake, I asked Ms. Thomas what she would advise anyone who wanted to go into the field of journalism and she stated, "Go for it! It's the greatest profession in the world because you are always learning and you are aware of the world, so you just might be able to affect change.

"You cannot have a democracy without an informed people.

"Information is everything; it enlarges your intellect and that guides you.

"The job is to follow the truth and report where it leads you!

"Right and wrong is not relative. Empathy is fine but kindness and sympathy do not change the facts and conscience is everything!

"Leaders are suppose to do the right thing and we should back up the president when he does the right thing; but drop him when he doesn't.

"The WHY is the most important question-not that something happened—but WHY did it happen?

"Somewhere along the way America lost its soul.

"People have to rise up but Americans have become so passive and power overwhelmingly abusive."

I responded, "So how do we fix this situation?"

Ms. Thomas readily replied, "It's being done!"

And when I asked Ms. Thomas if she had always wanted to be a journalist, her persistent smile broadened and the gleam in her eyes sparkled with unshed tears as she replied, "When my first article was published in the high school paper and I saw my byline, I was hooked!"

I shot back, "I had a similar but opposite experience!"

I explained that when I was a child, my dream was to grow up and become Brenda Starr, the red headed, ace investigative journalist and star reporter for the metropolitan daily, The Flash. The fictional Brenda traveled the world solving mysteries, unearthing scoops and she intuitively knew when somebody was not telling the truth.

But when my first assignment for the high school newspaper was edited beyond my recognition but my name was attached, my Irish temper erupted and I immediately confronted the faculty member on the paper and demanded, "Why did you publish an article with my name but with words I did NOT write?"

I was told that it was just standard procedure for the faculty to edit all of the student's work and I shot back, "Not mine you don't! I quit!"

Ms. Thomas pointed her finger at me and said, "That's ethics!"

And that comment is the second highest compliment I have ever been paid in my life!

The first remains the one Vanunu graced me with when he said, I was "always good to remind him of JC."

JC/Jesus Christ was never a Christian, but a social justice radical revolutionary nonviolent Palestinian devout Jew who rose up against a corrupt Temple and taught the people there was no need to pay the high priests for ritual baths or sacrificing livestock to be OK with God; for God already loved just as they were.

What got JC crucified was agitating the status quo of the Roman Occupying forces, for Rome's method of capitol punishment was to crucify all dissidents, rebels and agitators.

America was founded by visionaries, rebels, agitators, dissidents, fathers, mothers, sisters and brothers who essentially told the King of England to back off of this land and leave US alone. The most revolutionary minded of all America's founding fathers was Tom Paine, who articulated a flaming hope birthed in a vision of a new world driven by the spirit of independence from a British occupation.

Tom Paine's self published forty page pamphlet, "Common Sense" united a disparate and disconnected group of settlers to become compatriots who rose up in rebellion and formed a nation that can only thrive on dissent.

"Soon after I had published the pamphlet "Common Sense" [on Feb. 14, 1776] in America, I saw the exceeding probability that a revolution in the system of government would be followed by a revolution in the system of religion . . . The world is my country, all mankind are my brethren, and to do good is my religion."

Thomas Jefferson understood himself to be a true Christian and he proved so by remaining mute to the brutal and unjust accusations against him of being a deist, an atheist, anti-religion and antichrist.

Jefferson took Jesus so seriously, that he devoted twelve years of his life to literally cutting away all the miracle stories from the gospels in four different languages from the King James Bible and gluing all the passages of Jesus as a teacher and philosopher, onto pages that were bound between covers of straight-grain red morocco—a goat skin that is laboriously processed for over two months and tanned with sumac.

In 1902, Congressman John F. Lacey, a devout Christian, introduced a resolution for the printing of a facsimile of Jefferson's private piety to be distributed to Congress. Until the 1950's, every newly elected member of the Senate received a copy of "Jefferson's Bible" on the very day they swore their oath of office.

Lacey responded to the many critics who argued that stripping Jesus of his divinity was blasphemy: "No one that examines this little volume, whether he be saint or sinner, will rise from his perusal without having a loftier idea of the teachings of our Savior."

On his tombstone, Jefferson expressed that he wanted to be remembered as the Author of the Declaration of American Independence, the Statute of Virginia for Religious Freedom and the Father of the University of Virginia.

The ideas that were "self-evident" to America's Founding Fathers were the ideals of the Age of Enlightenment, which put forth the primacy of human reason, conscience and inherent human rights as it called for public education.

The inscription under the Dome of the Jefferson Memorial reads: "I have sworn upon the altar of god eternal hostility against every form of tyranny over the mind of man."

He wrote those words first to Dr. Benjamin Rush, in his search for a rational Christianity that could not be found in the corruptions, misconceptions, superstitions and "priest craft" that became self-evident in the days of Emperor Constantine with Augustine's JUST WAR heresy.

"You can't depend on your eyes when your IMAGINATION is out of focus."—Mark Twain

This will read like an urban legend, but it is fact that in 1945, in Egypt, in the land just above the bend of the Nile, north of the Valley of the Kings, across the river from the city of Nag´ Hammâdi, near the hamlet of al-Qasr, under a cliff called Jabal al-Tarif, an Egyptian Bedouin named Mohammed Ali was out gathering sabakh—a nitrate-rich fertilizer for the crops that he grew in the small hamlet of al-Qasr.

He was aghast to stumble upon a skeleton as he dug, and bewildered when he uncovered a two-foot high earthenware jar. A bowl had been placed over the top, and it was sealed with bitumen.

At first, the Bedouin thought an evil genie was within, but when he shook the heavy jar, he heard things moving and thought it might be gold. He smashed the jar open and out fluttered pieces of gold particles that he tried to catch, but they disappeared. When he peered into the jar, he was dismayed to find twelve leather-bound books.

Mohammed Ali was illiterate, so he placed no great value on books, but was confident he could sell them and make something for his troubles. So he carried the jar filled with books back to the homestead.

Now, Mohammed Ali also happened to be a fugitive from the law, for he had wielded the weapon that spilled the blood of a patriarch during a violent incident in a generation-long family feud, not so very long before.

After a few days of mulling over possibilities, he decided to give his find to the local Coptic priest for safekeeping. You see, he feared the authorities soon would be lurking about and would confiscate his possession before he could receive any money for it.

The priest passed it on to his brother-in-law, a traveling tutor, who brought the books to the Coptic museum in Cairo on October 4, 1946.

What was found were ancient compositions, written in Coptic that had been translated from ancient Greek. The volumes were leather-bound pages of papyrus, and no doubt the gold dust that Mohammed Ali witnessed was from papyrus fragments that had broken off.

Under the leadership of UNESCO, Egypt, and the American scholar James Robinson, these anthologies and collections of texts with titles like the Gospel of Thomas and the Gospel of Mary Magdalene have now been translated into many languages known as the Nag Hamadi Library.

These ancient texts offer NO new answers; but they do provide us with a glimpse of Christianity at its very roots, and it was most diverse indeed.

The most likely source for these books that have become known as the Nag Hamadi Library, was the Pachomius Monastery, which thrived for centuries just three miles from the burial site.

Scholars agree that most likely a monk from there buried these books in the wilderness under the cliff of Jabl al-Tarif for safekeeping.

These texts had been deemed heretical by those who were gaining power through the political arena; the Proto-orthodox.

In the 4th century, Emperor Constantine, a pagan warrior became the first Christian ruler, but waited until he was on his deathbed before being baptized.

I contend that the most decisive event in the history of Christendom occurred when Emperor Constantine accepted the Christian faith, for an earthly king now protected those who had once been persecuted.

Both a patriarchal monarchical state and church were formed at the same time. Power struggles and debates were common among the early Christians. Individual churches determined which texts were read, and they all had their favorites.

Constantine sought to unite his empire, and uniting the church was a savvy political move. He announced he would pay for fifty illuminated copies of scripture to be bound, and thus the biblical canon was established and sealed.

There was fierce debate among the bishops about what should be included and what left out. The proto-orthodox, who had now become the dominant voice, determined what was heretical for everyone. The proto-orthodox demanded much-loved scripture to be burned, usually because it did not fit their understanding of God.

Many of these texts were considered Gnostic, which is defined as knowledge discerned intuitively.

Gnostic texts offer deep mystery that is discerned via intuition, not rational thought.

This is not the way for fundamentalists.

A Gnostic is open to receiving intuitive knowledge of deep spiritual truth. For students of the New Testament, the Nag Hamadi Library is a much greater find than the Dead Sea Scrolls. Forty of the texts had previously been unknown to modern scholars.

Thirty-five scholars worked diligently on these translations, and all agreed that the bound books themselves date back to the fourth century and were written in Coptic translated from Greek and Aramaic-which is what Jesus spoke!

The Gospel of Thomas is a collection of the sayings of Jesus, words of wisdom, proverbs, parables, and some very confounding mysteries.

About 35 of the 114 sayings have no counterpart in the New Testament, while at least 20 are almost identical, and 54 have similarities.

Many scholars concur that the sayings were originally written in Syriac, a dialect of Aramaic, the language of Jesus and his followers.

It is very possible the sayings are closer to the words Jesus actually spoke than what is found in the canonical gospels.

Two thousand years ago, there was lively debate about who Jesus was, and why he came. The proto-orthodox, who were the majority, considered these Gnostic texts anathema and thus deemed them heretical for many reasons. The main reason is that they did not fit neatly into the evolving dogma.

Gnostic texts offer us mystery, not answers.

Jesus said he came that we would have life to the full; abundant life [John 10:10] and that takes deep thought.

I wonder what Dr. Rush and Thomas Jefferson would say to all of that?

What we do know is that Rush was raised in the evangelical "New Light" Presbyterian tradition of the 1730's. His faith laid emphasis on the individual's personal and emotional communion with God and those who shared his beliefs relied on the Bible and not the teachings of any clergymen.

Rush was also a Philadelphia physician, scientist and an active force in humanitarian efforts to end African American slavery.

Rush wrote, "The truths of Christianity dwell alike in the mind of the Deity, and reason and religion are equally the offspring of his goodness."

While watching Philly's Grand Procession to celebrate the U.S. Constitution in 1788, Rush saw what was a then a profoundly "American parade . . . a rabbi walked with arms linked between a Catholic priest and Protestant clergy-man."

Rush "always considered Christianity as the strong ground of Republicanism"—which is what we call democracy today.

In 1800, Rush wrote Jefferson, that this nation could only be steadied and the promise of the Revolution secured for future generations; if it is grounded in Christian morals and faith that are clarified by reason.

Jefferson's compatriot Thomas Paine who "saw the exceeding probability that a revolution in the system of government would be followed by a revolution in the system of religion" was soon condemned as the "ungodly author of THE AGE OF REASON" for offering God as creator while rejecting the divinity of Jesus and denouncing clerical power. Paine also wrote:

"A long habit of not thinking a thing wrong gives it a superficial appearance of being right."

"It is not a God, just and good, but a devil, under the name of God, that the Bible describes."

"Any system of religion that has anything in it that shocks the mind of a child cannot be true."

"Belief in a cruel God makes a cruel man."

"Every religion is good that teaches man to be good; and I know of none that instructs him to be bad."

"Is it not a species of blasphemy to call the New Testament revealed religion, when we see in it such contradictions and absurdities."

"Reason obeys itself; and ignorance submits to whatever is dictated to it."

"Reputation is what men and women think of us; character is what God and angels know of us."

I imagine God and the angels might agree with my Top Ten Teachings of Jesus as gleaned from THE JEFFERSON BIBLE:

1. Be just and justice comes from virtue, which comes from the heart.
2. Treat people the way you want to be treated.
3. Always work for PEACEFUL resolutions, even to the point of returning violence with COMPASSION.
4. Consider valuable the things that have no material value.
5. Do not judge others.
6. Do not bear grudges.
7. Be modest and unpretentious.
8. Give out of true generosity, not because one expects to be repaid or acknowledged.
9. Being true to one's self in more important than being loyal to one's family and following ones conscience is the only way to do it.
10. Those who think they know the most are the most ignorant.

In "A Bill for Establishing Religious Freedom", Jefferson wrote:

"Well aware that the opinions and belief of men depend not on their own will, but follow involuntarily the evidence proposed to their minds; that Almighty God hath created the mind free, and manifested his supreme will that free it shall remain by making it altogether insusceptible of restraint; that all attempts to influence it by temporal punishments, or burthens, or by civil incapacitations, tend only to beget habits of hypocrisy and meanness, and are a departure from the plan of the holy author of our religion.

"God who gave us life gave us liberty. Can the liberties of a nation be secure when we have removed a conviction that these liberties are the gift of God? Indeed I tremble for my country when I reflect that God is just, that his justice cannot sleep forever. Commerce between master and slave is despotism. Nothing is more certainly written in the book of fate than that these people are to be free. Establish a law for educating the common people. This it is the business of the state and on a general plan.

"I am certainly not an advocate for frequent and untried changes in laws and constitutions. I think moderate imperfections had better be borne with; because, when once known, we accommodate ourselves to them, and find practical means of correcting their ill effects. But I know also, that laws and institutions must go hand in hand with the progress of the human mind. As that becomes more developed, more enlightened, as new discoveries are made, new truths disclosed, and manners and opinions change with the change of circumstances, institutions must advance also, and keep pace with the times. We might as well require a man to wear still the coat which fitted him when a boy, as civilized society to remain ever under the regimen of their barbarous ancestors."

If we truly "hold these truths to be self-evident: That all [people] are created equal; that they are endowed by their creator with certain unalienable rights . . . that, to secure these rights, governments are instituted among [people] deriving their just powers from the consent of the governed; and, whenever any form of government becomes destructive of these ends, it is the RIGHT of the people to ALTER or to ABOLISH it" we will also realize the simple truth that Governments have obligations but people have rights.

Among our rights comes the obligation to hold our Government accountable for their actions as well as holding politicians accountable for failures to keep their promises.

I IMAGINE if all who claim to be Christian meditate [think!] upon "The Life and Morals of Jesus of Nazareth by Thomas Jefferson" my spin on The Sermon on The Mount-the Christian Manifesto would be just one of many spun in the 21st century about Jesus of Nazareth.

When Jesus was about 33, he hiked up a hill and sat down under an olive tree and began to teach the people strange things, such as "Blessed are the poor in spirit, for theirs is the Kingdom of heaven."

In other words: it is those who know their own spiritual poverty, their own limitations and 'sins' honestly and trust God loves them in spite of themselves who already live in the Kingdom of God.

How comforted we will all be, when we see, we haven't got a clue, as to the depth and breadth of pure love and mercy of The Divine Mystery of The Universe.

God's name in ancient Aramaic is Abba, which means Daddy, as much as Mommy and He/She: The Lord has said, "My ways are not your ways. My thoughts are not yours."—Isaiah 55:8

Christ proclaimed more: "Blessed are the meek, for they shall inherit the earth."

The essence of meek is to be patient with ignorance, slow to anger and never hold a grudge. In other words: how comforted you will be when you also know humility; when you know yourself, the good and the bad, for both cut through every human heart.

"Blessed are those who hunger and thirst for righteousness, they will be filled."

In other words: how comforted you will be when your greatest desire is to do what "God requires, and he has already told you what that is; BE JUST, BE MERCIFUL and walk humbly with your Lord."-Micah 6:8

"Blessed are the merciful, they will be shown mercy." In other words: how comforted you will all be when you choose to return only kindness to your 'enemy.'

"For with the measure you measure against another, it will be measured back to you" Christ warns his disciples as he explains the law of karma in Luke 6:27-38.

"Blessed are the pure in heart, for they see God."

In other words: how comforted you will be when you WAKE UP and see God is already within you, within every man, every woman and every child. The Supreme Being is everywhere, the Alpha and Omega, beginning and end. Beyond The Universe—and yet so small; within the heart of every atom.

"Blessed are The Peacemakers: THEY shall be called the children of God."

And what a wonderful world it would be when we all seek peace by pursuing justice; for there can be none without the other.

"Think left and think right. Think low and think high. Oh the thinks you can think up. If only you try."—Dr. Suess

My run for congress was always more an exercise for experience than a possibility of a win, so I was surprised and heart warmed that 7,837 individuals cast their vote for me to be their US HOUSE of Representative. I was running against a republican, Tea-Party Christian Zionist, who promoted herself as "the Christian values leader" and the now 11th term career incumbent, democrat Corrine Brown. "The Christian values leader" ran on a platform of support for Israel and against same sex marriage. Brown has yet to publicly commit to a position on either.

During the campaign season, a group of conservative pastors in central Florida invited the US House candidates to respond to their "faith based" questions. When they asked me where I stood regarding same sex marriage, I replied, "God is love and the way any two people share love is between them and God. It is not the business of the State who should or shouldn't marry, but it is the right of religious institutions to bless-or not-any union. But God is love and wherever love is-God is already there and has already blessed that union."

"The Christian values leader" received the conservative pastors endorsement and I was most gleeful for the opportunity to attend the 'inquisition' just to provoke some thought. Another way I attempt to do that, is to seize opportunities to mention to American Christians that two thousand years ago The Cross had NO symbolic religious meaning and was not a piece of jewelry. When Jesus said, "Pick up your cross and follow me," everyone back then understood he was issuing a POLITICAL statement—for the main roads in Jerusalem were lined with crucified agitators, rebels, dissidents and any others who disturbed the status quo of the Roman Occupying Forces. In response, most American Christians just look perplexed; but Palestinian Christians and Muslims always relate.

Corrine Brown has been a member of the US House of Representatives since 1993. In June 2012, I attempted to engage Corrine Brown in a civilized conversation on her Face Book Wall. Brown responded in an attempt to CENSOR me by DELETING my comments and BLOCKING me from adding more. One of the comments Brown censored was regarding the "Eat and Greet" all state and federal candidates had been invited to in Sanford, Fl. on June 11th.

Brown did not attend or send a representative, but I schlepped over an hour to offer 'concerned citizens' reams of information about the 45th Anniversary of USS Liberty Attack and all about the money that we the people who pay taxes in this nation are being forced to pay to prolong an immoral, illegal and untenable 45 years of Military Occupation of the indigenous Palestinians. [The info came courtesy of US Campaign to End the Israeli Occupation]

While my two-minute introduction was well received, I got shot down immediately by the 'concerned citizens' when I brought up the Occupation of Palestine! Everyone believed that God had made a real estate deal with the ancient Hebrews, but all were clueless that the deal was contingent upon the ancients upholding their end of the bargain!

As the Zionist Rabbi Michael Lerner teaches, "From Moses to Jeremiah and Isaiah, the Prophets taught, that the Jewish claim on the land of Israel was totally contingent on the moral and spiritual life of the Jews who lived there, and that the land would, as the Torah tells us, 'vomit you out' if people did not live according to the highest moral vision of Torah. Over and over again, the Torah repeated its most frequently stated mitzvah [command]: When you enter your land, do not oppress the stranger; the other, the one who is an outsider of your society, the powerless one and then not only 'you shall love your neighbor as yourself' but also 'you shall love the other.'" [TIKKUN Magazine, page 35, Sept./Oct. 2007]

The First Amendment of The CONSTITUTION upholds Freedom of Religion and that Congress has NO RIGHT to prohibit "the free exercise thereof; or abridging the freedom of speech, or of the press; or the right of the people peaceably to assemble, and to petition the Government for a redress of grievances."

Thus, I continue my fervent battle to provoke the 'Christian' Zionists in this Government to THINK; because there is nothing Christ-like about Zionism!

Christian Zionism is an extremist Christian movement, which supports the claims of those who believe that the State of Israel should take control of all of the land currently disputed between Palestinians and Israelis. It views the creation and expansion of the modern state of Israel as a fulfillment of biblical prophecy toward the second coming of Jesus. Christian Zionism is a modern theological and political movement that embraces the most extreme ideological positions of Zionism, thereby becoming detrimental to a just peace within Palestine and Israel.

The Christian Zionist program provides a worldview where the Gospel is identified with the ideology of empire, colonialism and militarism. In its extreme form, it laces an emphasis on apocalyptic events leading to the end of history rather than living Christ's love and justice today.

Believing that God fights on the side of Israel, Christian Zionists call for the unqualified support for the most extreme political positions. They do not have eyes to see or ears to hear their sisters and brothers in Christ, or cousins in the family of Father Abraham who are caught in the crossfire of the military minded.

Christian Zionist spokespersons have also attributed Hurricane Katrina to God's wrath over America's failure to stop Israel from "disengaging" from Gaza in 2005, although Israel has never ceased their total control over air, land and sea borders!

Christian Zionism has significant support within American Protestant fundamentalists, and number between 10 and 20 million. Its reach is broad, by virtue of its favorite themes related to the "End Times" and an Israel-fixated Christian media.

Christian Zionism is both a political movement and a way of misinterpreting current events. Its focus on Israel and the Middle East is an ideology and a movement. Its promoters share many beliefs but are not organized through any one institution.

Throughout history Christians have at times twisted scripture to justify violence: for the Crusades, for Antisemitism, and for slavery. Too often the Church has been slow to respond to these biblical distortions and with disastrous results. Today Christian Zionists—particularly those with dispensationalist leanings—are well organized and although their motives are couched in terms of compassion toward the Jewish people they base their theology on literal readings of scripture.

The political agenda of territorial expansion advocated by Christian Zionists has given rise to the brutal injustices against Palestinians, which fuels the fires of militancy in the Middle East and they also consistently oppose any moves towards a solution to the conflict, which would validate the political aspirations of both Palestinians and Israelis.

While Jewish Zionism began with the hope that all Jewish people would have a safe and peaceful dwelling place, these corruptors of the gospel Christ preached, adhere to a 200 year old convoluted interpretation of disparate scriptures that they have chosen to weave together to support their fear based judgmental narrow minded doctrine.

The heretical theology of Premellenial Dispensation worships a god of Armageddon and not the God of love, forgiveness and compassion that Jesus/The Prince of Peace modeled even while being nailed to a cross. The "Left Behind" series of fiction is the epitome of what millennium of theologians have always understood to be what the term anti-Christ is truly about.

The term "Antichrist" only appears five times in the Bible, but a cult not based on sound theology has created an urban legend that seeks Armageddon. The term "Antichrist" never appears in John's Revelation or Daniel, two disparate works of literature written three centuries apart and under very different circumstances, yet the Left Behinder's weave them together.

The small texts that mention the "Antichrist" were written to attack the Gnostic understanding of whom Christ was. A Gnostic relies on intuition and not on dogma and doctrine. Gnostic's were most certainly free spirits and most all of the writings we have about Gnostics, have been the attacks upon them. That all changed when the Nag Hamadi Library was translated and published, for what had been deemed heretical by those in power in the fourth century can now be read in most every language.

Biblical scholars today agree that many books of the Bible were written by others in the name of an apostle, for the quickest way to gain credibility is to trade on another's reputation. We may never know if the author who coined the term "Antichrist" was actually the apostle John who wrote I John and 2 John-the only sources where the term appears. John also say's:

"Dear Children, as you have heard that the Antichrist is coming, even now many have come."—I John 2:18

"This is how we know who the children of God are not: anyone who does not do right; nor anyone who does not love his brother."-I John 3:10

"If anyone has material possessions and sees his brother in need but has no pity on him, how can the love of God be in him? Let us love with actions and in truth."-I John 3:17

"God is love. Whoever lives in love lives in God, and God in him. There is no fear in love. Perfect love drives out all fear because fear has to do with punishment [and God is love]."-1 John 4:18

The theology promoted in the "Left Behind" fiction is a theology based on fear and punishment. The "Left Behind" Christians worship a punitive father as God and they do not have eyes to see that nature is God's primary temple, and war the greatest abomination. The theology of the fictional "Left Behind" series is the epitome of the spirit of the anti-Christ: which is the evil within ones own heart that leads one to fear "the other" and compels them to violence.

According to Christ, to be his follower, one must do what the Father requires. The Hebrew prophet Micah summed it up best: "What does the Lord require? He has already told you o'man: Be Just, Be Merciful and walk humbly with your God."—Micah 6:8:

To be just is to be fair and reasonable. To be merciful means to treat all people the way we want to be treated. To be humble is knowing oneself; the good and the evil, for both cut through every human heart. Jesus taught that the only way to resist evil is with good and to always work for peaceful resolutions, even to the point of returning violence with compassion and forgiveness.

Knowledge can be gotten from books. Wisdom observes, forgives but never forgets.

"Imagination is the voice of daring. If there is anything Godlike about God it is that. He dared to imagine everything."—Henry Miller

In 1987, Vanunu, wrote from Ashkelon prison:

"No government, not even the most democratic, can force us to live under this threat. No state in the world can offer any kind of security against this menace of a nuclear holocaust, or guarantee to prevent it. A state that lives in fear of destruction must not threaten the whole world with annihilation.

"Any country, which manufactures and stocks nuclear weapons, is first of all endangering its own citizens. This is why the citizens must confront their government and warn it that it has no right to expose them to this danger. Because, in effect, the citizens are being held hostage by their own government, just as if they have been hijacked and deprived of their freedom and threatened.

"When governments develop nuclear weapons without the consent of their citizens—and this is true in most cases—they are violating the basic rights of their citizens, the basic right not to live under constant threat of annihilation . . . Is any government qualified and authorized to produce such weapons?"

The answer has always been NO!

On 5 April 2009, President Obama stood on the world stage in Prague amongst thousands of flag-waving Czechs and spoke of good humor, home town Chicago, the will of the people over tanks and guns, old conflicts, revolution, moral leadership as the most powerful weapon, iron curtains that fell and the state of 21st century nuclear weapons. An excerpt:

"We are here today because enough people ignored the voices who told them that the world could not change. We're here today because of the courage of those who stood up and took risks to say that freedom is a right for all people, no matter what side of a wall they live on, and no matter what they look like. We are here today because the simple and principled pursuit of liberty and opportunity shamed those who relied on the power of tanks and arms to put down the will of a people.

"Some argue that the spread of these weapons cannot be stopped, cannot be checked—that we are destined to live in a world where more nations and more people possess the ultimate tools of destruction. Such fatalism is a deadly adversary, for if we believe that the spread of nuclear weapons is inevitable, then in some way we are admitting to ourselves that the use of nuclear weapons is inevitable.

"As the only nuclear power to have used a nuclear weapon, the United States has a moral responsibility to act . . . It will take patience and persistence. But now we, too, must ignore the voices who tell us that the world cannot change. We have to insist, Yes, we can.

"There is violence and injustice in our world that must be confronted. We must confront it by standing together as free nations, as free people. I know that a call to arms can stir the souls of men and women more than a call to lay them down. But that is why the voices for peace and progress must be raised together.

"Human destiny will be what we make of it . . . Let us honor our past by reaching for a better future. Let us bridge our divisions, build upon our hopes, and accept our responsibility to leave this world more prosperous and more peaceful than we found it. Together we can do it.

"Words must mean something."

Agreed and inspired by the words of Rev. Martin Luther King from Birmingham Jail, which directly challenged his "fellow clergymen" I seized a few liberties to spin it as a Citizens of Conscience Manifesto in my run for US House:

I am on the Internet because injustice can be expressed here. I am cognizant of the interrelatedness of all communities and states. I cannot sit idly by in comfort and not be concerned about what happens in Israel Gaza Palestine.

Injustice anywhere is a threat to justice everywhere. We are caught in an inescapable network of mutuality, tied in a single garment of destiny. Whatever affects one directly, affects all indirectly. Never again can we afford to live with the narrow, provincial "outside agitator" idea. Anyone who lives in the world can never be considered an outsider anywhere within its bounds.

In any nonviolent campaign there are four basic steps: collection of the facts to determine whether injustices exist; negotiation; examining one's motives and acting on conscience with direct action.

Nonviolent direct action seeks to create such a crisis and foster such a tension that a community, which has constantly refused to negotiate, is forced to confront the issue. It seeks so to dramatize the issue that it can no longer be ignored I am not afraid of the word "tension." I have earnestly opposed violent tension, but there is a type of constructive, nonviolent tension, which is necessary for growth.

Too long has The Peace Process been bogged down in a tragic effort to live in monologue rather than dialogue.

Lamentably, it is an historical fact that privileged groups seldom give up their privileges voluntarily. We know through painful experience that freedom is never voluntarily given by the oppressor; it must be demanded by the oppressed. We must come to see that "justice too long delayed is justice denied."

There are two types of laws: just and unjust. I would be the first to advocate obeying just laws. One has not only a legal but also a moral responsibility to obey just laws. Conversely, one has a moral responsibility to disobey unjust laws. I would agree with St. Augustine "an unjust law is no law at all."

A just law is a man made code that squares with the moral law or the law of God. An unjust law is a code that is out of harmony with the moral law. To put it in the terms of St. Thomas Aquinas: An unjust law is a human law that is not rooted in eternal law and natural law. Any law that uplifts human personality is just. Any law that degrades human personality is unjust.

Segregation [Translates to Apartheid in Afrikaner] distorts the soul and damages the personality. It gives the segregator a false sense of superiority and the segregated a false sense of inferiority. Segregation, to use the terminology of the Jewish philosopher Martin Buber, substitutes an "I it" relationship for an "I thou" relationship and ends up relegating persons to the status of things.

Hence segregation; apartheid, conscription and military occupation is not only politically, economically and sociologically unsound; it is morally wrong and sinful. Paul Tillich has said that sin is separation. Is not segregation an existential expression of man's tragic separation, his awful estrangement, his terrible sinfulness?

An unjust law is a code that a numerical or power majority group compels a minority group to obey but does not make binding on itself. This is difference made legal. By the same token, a just law is a code that a majority compels a minority to follow and that it is willing to follow itself. This is sameness made legal.

One who breaks an unjust law must do so openly, lovingly, and with a willingness to accept the penalty. I submit that an individual who breaks a law that conscience tells him is unjust, and who willingly accepts the penalty of imprisonment in order to arouse the conscience of the community over its injustice, is in reality expressing the highest respect for law.

Everything Adolf Hitler did in Germany was "legal" and it was "illegal" to aid and comfort a Jew in Hitler's Germany.

Shallow understanding from people of good will is more frustrating than absolute misunderstanding from people of ill will. Lukewarm acceptance is much more bewildering than outright rejection.

Oppressed people cannot remain oppressed forever and if repressed emotions are not released in nonviolent ways, they will seek expression through violence; this is not a threat but a fact of history. [End of Letter from Birmingham Jail]

In his Letter from Birmingham Jail, King reminded his fellow clergymen that Jesus was an extremist for love who taught his follower's to "Love your enemies, bless them that curse you, do good to them that hate you, and pray for them which despitefully use you, and persecute you."

King recalled to his fellow clerics that the Hebrew prophet Amos was an extremist for justice: "Let justice roll down like waters and righteousness like an ever flowing stream."

The world is pulled to change by extremism and our only dilemma is what will we be extremists for? Hate or love? God or State? The preservation of injustice or the extension of justice; equal human rights?

The clinging to the status quo is a form of extremism for all around US are the deep groans from the oppressed, as King addressed from his jail cell:

Few members of the oppressor race can understand the deep groans and passionate yearnings of the oppressed race, and still fewer have the vision to see that injustice must be rooted out by strong, persistent and determined action. Too many others have been more cautious than courageous and have remained silent behind the anesthetizing security of stained glass windows.

There was a time when the church was very powerful—in the time when the early Christians rejoiced at being deemed worthy to suffer for what they believed. In those days the church was not merely a thermometer that recorded the ideas and principles of popular opinion; it was a thermostat that transformed the mores of society. Whenever the early Christians entered a town, the people in power became disturbed and immediately sought to convict the Christians for being "disturbers of the peace" and "outside agitators."'

Small in number, they were big in commitment and by their effort and example they brought an end to such ancient evils as infanticide and gladiatorial contests. Things are different now. So often the contemporary church is a weak, ineffectual voice with an uncertain sound. So often it is an arch defender of the status quo. Far from being disturbed by the presence of the church, the power structure of the average community is consoled by the church's silent—and often even vocal—sanction of things as they are.

If today's church does not recapture the sacrificial spirit of the early church, it will lose its authenticity, forfeit the loyalty of millions, and be dismissed as an irrelevant social club with no meaning for the twenty-first century.

King wondered if organized religion was too inextricably bound to the status quo to save our nation and the world. He knew that "Any nation that year after year continues to raise the Defense budget while cutting social programs to the neediest is a nation approaching spiritual death."

We who claim to be Christian are called to love our enemies and that the daughters and sons of God are the peacemakers. The last words Jesus spoke to his follower's before his martyrdom was to "put down the sword" and his first words after his resurrection was "My peace be with you."

During one of my seven trips to occupied Palestine since 2005, Mohammad Alatar, film producer of "The Ironwall" addressed my group on an Israeli Committee Against House Demolitions tour through Jerusalem and to the village of Anata and the Shufat refugee camp, in the very area where the prophet Jeremiah in the 6th century B.C. critiqued the violent conflicts in the Mid East, which were already old news: "I hear

violence and destruction in the city, sickness and wounds are all I see."
[Jeremiah 6:7]

After we broke bread and ate a typical Palestinian feast prepared by the
Arabiya family in the Arabyia Peace Center, Mohammad Alatar said:

"I am a Muslim Palestinian American and when my son asked me who my
hero was I took three days to think about it. I told him my hero is Jesus,
because he took a stand and he died for it. What really needs to be done
is for the churches to be like Jesus; to challenge the Israeli occupation
and address the apartheid practices as moral issues. Even if every church
divested and boycotted Israel it would not harm Israel. After the USA and
Russia, Israel is the third largest arms exporter in the world. It is a moral
issue that the churches must address."

While he lived the FBI placed wiretaps on Reverend King's home and
office phones and bugged his hotel rooms throughout the country. By
1967, King had become the country's most prominent opponent of the
Vietnam War, and a staunch critic of U.S. foreign policy, which he deemed
militaristic.

In his "Beyond Vietnam" speech delivered at New York's Riverside Church
on April 4, 1967 [a year to the day before he was murdered] King called
the United States "the greatest purveyor of violence in the world today."

In 1986 the federal government 'honored' King with a national holiday.

"Fuck hope! It's not about hope. You don't do what you do because you hope things will get better. It's about getting up every morning and asking yourself what's the right thing to do and doing it."—Allen Ginsburg

In a November 7, 2012, Press release, "AIPAC applauded the election of a solidly pro-Israel Congress. Tuesday's results reflect that the firm bond between America and the Jewish state has become even stronger. Once again, the American people have demonstrated with their votes that the US-Israel friendship transcends partisan politics. At a time of heightened partisan polarization, candidates from both parties expressed unanimity in their support for Israel's security. While there has been a very high turnover of members of the Senate and the House over the past few election cycles, there remains an extraordinary continuity of unwavering solidarity with Israel by both incumbents and challengers. Virtually all the candidates who were elected issued position papers and statements expressing their belief that Israel is an invaluable ally of America. The voice of the American people was heard yesterday and they made it unambiguously clear that the US and Israel are united by an unbreakable bond. We welcome the incoming Congress and look forward to working with them and President Obama to strengthen the relationship between America and Israel—the one nation in the volatile Middle East that shares our democratic values and beliefs."

In his Farewell Address, George Washington warned, "Sympathy for the favorite nation, facilitating the illusion of an imaginary common interest in cases where no real common interest exists, and infusing into one the enmities of the other, betrays the former in the quarrels and wars of the latter, without adequate justification."

Another reason I wanted to serve in the US HOUSE was to be a countervailing force against the lock step mentality of Israel first, which puts this homeland in jeopardy. If I had been elected, I would have gifted my peers with copies of "Foreign Agents: The American Israel Public Affairs Committee from the 1963 Fulbright Hearings to the 2005 Espionage Scandal" written by Grant F. Smith, the Director for the Institute of Research Middle East Policy.

Smith explained how America's Middle East policy has been formulated and thrives due to the dearth of relevant reporting on AIPAC's activities—essentially because the old Fourth Estate has acted more like Sayanim [VOLUNTEERS] for Zionism than muckrakers—meaning investigative journalists!

Before the worn out canard of being an "Anti-Semite" is hurled at me—again—I reiterate that TRUE Anti-Semitism is a prejudice against or hostility towards the Jewish people which is rooted in fear which breed's hatred and it must be denounced and confronted!

Case In Point: In my first book, "KEEP HOPE ALIVE" I wrote through the fictional character Jack Hunt regarding the 'Christian' Crusades and the Jewish Holocaust:

"Those barbarians tortured and burned people at the stake! What kind of Christian could rationalize that? So much hypocrisy! I will not give my soul over to another. No institution is going to control me. I think Christians can be real cowards, or else they were sleeping while Hitler was gaining power. I hate to think it, but maybe it was because they were anti-Semitic?"

According to Webster's Dictionary a SEMITE is "a member of any of a number of peoples of ancient southwestern Asia including the Akkadians, Phoenicians, Hebrews, and Arabs or a descendant of these peoples" thus Palestinians are as much a Semite as any Jew!

So let us move on by going back to the days when Senator Fulbright asked questions regarding Jewish-Agency-funded US foreign agents who did not register with the Justice Department or disclose their true financing, funding flows or covert activities and how AIPAC/American Israel Public Affairs Committee operates "within a murky nexus regulated by four important but seldom enforced US laws."

The lax enforcement of The Logan Act, The Foreign Agents Registration Act/FARA, the 1917 Espionage Act, Thompson Memorandum guidelines for prosecuting corporate crime coupled with the fear of being labeled anti-Semitic and a media who have failed at their commission to seek and report the truth have all colluded to exert an undue influence over Congress and thus; we the people of America to be "under the de facto influence of a powerful foreign interest."

AIPAC is a constellation of individuals and organizations that make up the "Israel lobby" and I define as the Zionist Lobby, which actively steers USA foreign policy in a militant and pro-Israel only direction.

Senator Fulbright expressed great concern over the activities of unregistered foreign agents who worked to influence public opinion and policy which resulted in the 1963 Senate Foreign Relations Committee hearings which investigated and uncovered a "conduit" operation run by the American Zionist Council, which in 1959 was renamed AIPAC.

Within eight years, the American Zionist Council had received over a half a million from the Jewish Agency to create a favorable opinion in this country for Israeli government policies. The Senate investigation closed down the conduit, but the extensive propaganda activities still go on and by 1998, US aid to Israel exceeded $3 billion a year, the highest amount of US aid given to any country.

In 2002, Harvard economist Thomas Stauffer estimated the total cost of the Israeli Palestinian conflict at $3 trillion and he laid a good deal of the blame for that at the doorstep of AIPAC.

There is also the money laundering of over 50 billion US dollars to "charitable" organizations and massive covert activities that have enabled the ongoing building of the apartheid Israeli settlements, which have expropriated legally owned Palestinian land. Today a quarter of a million Jewish settlers/colonists-most all of which have no historical tie to the Holy Land, have created 'facts on the ground' to disable a viable contiguous Palestinian state.

On November 21, 2005, top U.S. law enforcement officials attended a briefing organized by the Council for the National Interest regarding how charities such as B'nai B'rith and Hadassah were in direct control of the World Zionist Organization and directly linked to a massive money-laundering operation. The settlements are also an indirect generator of terrorism against the United States. Israel has also never signed the Nuclear Non-Proliferation treaty, which prohibits U.S. assistance to any country trafficking in nuclear enrichment's equipment or technology outside of international safeguards. The World is well aware of Israel's clandestine nuclear weapons development, stockpile, and launch capabilities, but due to the influence of AIPAC, criminal wrongdoing corrupts America's core values and the media helps shift Middle East policy to focus on Iran, which has not threatened America! In fact, in 2006, Virginia Tilley a Professor of political science explained:

"In his October 2005 speech, Mr. Ahmadinejad never used the word 'map' or the term 'wiped off.' According to Farsi-language experts like Juan Cole and even right-wing services like MEMRI, what he actually said was 'this regime that is occupying Jerusalem must vanish from the page of time.'

"In this speech to an annual anti-Zionist conference, Mr. Ahmadinejad was being prophetic, not threatening. He was citing Imam Khomeini, who said this line in the 1980s-a period when Israel was actually selling arms to Iran, so apparently it was not viewed as so ghastly then.

"Mr. Ahmadinejad had just reminded his audience that the Shah's regime, the Soviet Union, and Saddam Hussein had all seemed enormously powerful and immovable, yet the first two had vanished almost beyond recall and the third now languished in prison.

"So, too, the 'occupying regime' in Jerusalem would someday be gone. His message was, in essence: 'This too shall pass.'"

What has yet to pass are international atomic agency inspectors into Israel's WMD facility and honest brokering for Middle East Peace with Justice! In 1976, the Symington Amendment was adopted to fortify and extend the Nuclear Non-Proliferation Treaty. It prohibited US assistance to any country trafficking in nuclear enrichment equipment or technology outside of international safeguards.

On October 5, 1986, the world learned about Israel's secret underground nuclear weapons facility when many of Mordechai Vanunu's photographs from top secret locations in Dimona, accompanied by his testimony as a mid level nuclear technician were published by the London Sunday Times.

A few elephants in the world include US collusion in Israel's policy of Nuclear Ambiguity [the politically correct euphemism for Nuclear Deceptions] and Nuclear Apartheid. Add in Israel's defiance of international law and UN resolutions and it is no stretch of imagination to imagine the instability in the Middle East will remain a tinderbox until American policy changes.

Jonathan Ben Artzi, [nephew of Israeli Prime Minister Benjamin Netanyahu, who spent eighteen months in jail for refusing to serve in the IDF as a conscientious objector against the Israeli Occupation of Palestine] pleaded, "Sometimes it takes a good friend to tell you when enough is enough. As they did with South Africa two decades ago, concerned citizens across the US can make a difference by encouraging Washington to get the message to Israel that this cannot continue. If Americans truly are our friends, they should shake us up and take away the keys, because right now we are driving drunk, and without this wake-up call, we will soon find ourselves in the ditch of an undemocratic, doomed state."

But, beginning in the 1990's and even more so after 9/11, US politicians blind allegiance to Israel has been furthered by the refrain that both states are threatened by Arab terrorist groups and rogue states bent on acquiring weapons of mass destruction. Many Americans see Israel as an ally and Iran as a mutual enemy, but I recall Pogo from the 1960's, "We have seen the enemy and he is US!"

Unless a 2013 federal budget is passed, discretionary spending programs, including U.S. military aid to Israel, will be cut across-the-board through the process known formally as "sequestration" and referred to as the "fiscal cliff."

If a budget is passed, Israel will continue to receive their annual $3.1 billion in regular military aid, plus up to $950 million more in anti-missile projects—'courtesy' of the American taxpayer, who would be wise to reject the worn out canard, "Israel is our only democratic ally in the Middle East" because it is incongruent with 21st century realities.

"The age of warrior kings and of warrior presidents has passed. The nuclear age calls for a different kind of leadership; a leadership of intellect, judgment, tolerance and rationality, a leadership committed to human values, to world peace, and to the improvement of the human condition. The attributes upon which we must draw are the human attributes of compassion and common sense, of intellect and creative imagination, and of empathy and understanding between cultures."—William Fulbright

The "war on terror" has become a tactic to infuse fear while it ignores that much of the anger in the Arab world is in response to Israel's military occupation of Palestine and The Wall which has been built on legally owned Palestinian property and financed with U.S. aid at a cost of over $1.5 million per mile. The Wall prevents residents from receiving health care, emergency medical services and separates farmers from their olive groves, which have been their families' sole livelihood for generations.

In July 2012, an official Israeli-government appointed commission concluded that the Fourth Geneva Convention does not apply to Israel's military occupation of the Palestinian West Bank, East Jerusalem and Gaza Strip because, claiming that Israel is not actually engaged in a military occupation and therefore the convention's prohibition against colonizing occupied territory does not apply.

In October 2012, a public opinion poll of Jewish Israelis found that 47% support the ethnic cleansing of Palestinian citizens of Israel. 58% believe Israel practices apartheid toward Palestinians, and 69% favor denying Palestinians the right to vote if Israel annexes the West Bank.

Haaretz columnist Danny Rubinstein was quoted in a UN report, "Israel today was an apartheid State with four different Palestinian groups: those in Gaza, East Jerusalem, the West Bank and Israeli Palestinians, each of which had a different status . . . even if the wall followed strictly the line of the pre-1967 border, it would still not be justified. The two peoples needed cooperation rather than walls because they must be neighbors."

An apartheid society is much more than just a 'settler colony'. It involves specific forms of oppression that actively strip the original inhabitants of any rights at all, whereas civilian members of the invader caste are given all kinds of sumptuous privileges.

On May 14, 1948, The Declaration of the establishment of Israel affirmed that, "The State of Israel will be based on freedom, justice and peace as envisaged by the prophets of Israel: it will ensure complete equality of social and political rights to all its inhabitants irrespective of religion it will guarantee freedom of religion [and] conscience and will be faithful to the Charter of the United Nations."

However, reality intrudes, for "The truth, which is known to all; through its army, the government of Israel practices a brutal form of Apartheid in the territory it occupies. Its army has turned every Palestinian village and town into a fenced-in, or blocked-in, detention camp."—Israeli Minister of Education, Shulamit Aloni quoted in the popular Israeli newspaper, Yediot Acharonot on December 20, 2006.

How could a state founded on "equality of social and political rights to all its inhabitants" come to be such a state of hypocrisy?

A Little History:

On July 5, 1950, Israel enacted the Law of Return by which Jews anywhere in the world, have a "right" to immigrate to Israel on the grounds that they are returning to their own state, even if they nor their families have ever been there before.

On July 14, 1952: The enactment of the Citizenship/Jewish Nationality Law, results in Israel becoming the only state in the world to grant a particular national-religious group—the Jews—the right to settle in it and gain automatic citizenship.

In 1953, South Africa's Prime Minister Daniel Malan became the first foreign head of government to visit Israel and returns home with the message that Israel can be a source of inspiration for white South Africans.

In 1962, South African Prime Minister Verwoerd declared that Jews "took Israel from the Arabs after the Arabs had lived there for a thousand years. In that I agree with them, Israel, like South Africa, is an apartheid state."

On August 1, 1967, Israel enacted the Agricultural Settlement Law, which bans Israeli citizens of non-Jewish nationality [Palestinian Arabs] from working on Jewish National Fund lands, which is over 80% of the land in Israel.

Knesset member Uri Avnery stated: "This law is going to expel Arab cultivators from the land that was formerly theirs and was handed over to the Jews."

On April 4, 1969, General Moshe Dayan is quoted in the Israeli newspaper Ha'aretz telling students at Israel's Technion Institute that "Jewish villages were built in the place of Arab villages. You don't even know the names of these Arab villages, and I don't blame you, because these geography books no longer exist. Not only do the books not exist, the Arab villages are not there either . . . There is not one single place built in this country that did not have a former Arab population."

On April 28, 1971: C. L. Sulzberger, writing in The New York Times, quoted South African Prime Minister John Vorster as saying that Israel is faced with an apartheid problem, namely how to handle its Arab inhabitants. "Both South Africa and Israel are in a sense intruder states. They were built by pioneers originating abroad and settling in partially inhabited areas."

Vanunu's WAIT for Liberty

On September 13, 1978, in Washington, D.C. The Camp David Accords are signed by Egyptian President Anwar Sadat and Israeli Prime Minister Menachem Begin and witnessed by President Jimmy Carter.

The Accords reaffirm U.N. Resolutions 242 and 338, which prohibit acquisition of land by force, call for Israel's withdrawal of military and civilian forces from the West Bank and Gaza, and prescribe "full autonomy" for the inhabitants of the territories.

Prime Minister Begin promises President Carter that he will freeze all settlement activity during the subsequent peace talks. Once back in Israel, however, Israel continues to confiscate, settle, and fortify the occupied territories.

On September 13, 1985, Rep. George Crockett (D-MI), after visiting the Israeli-occupied West Bank, compares the living conditions there with those of South African blacks and concludes that the West Bank is an instance of apartheid that no one in the U.S. is talking about.

In July 2000, President Bill Clinton convenes the Camp David II Peace Summit between Israeli Prime Minister Ehud Barak and Palestinian Authority Chairman Yasser Arafat. Clinton—not Barak—offers Arafat the withdrawal of some 40,000 Jewish settlers, leaving more than 180,000 in 209 settlements, all of which are interconnected by roads that cover approximately 10% of the occupied land.

Effectively, this divides the West Bank into at least two non-contiguous areas and multiple fragments. Palestinians would have no control over the borders around them, the air space above them, or the water reserves under them. Barak calls it a generous offer. Arafat refuses to sign.

On August 31, 2001, in Durban, South Africa, up to 50,000 South Africans march in support of the Palestinian people. In their "Declaration by South Africans on Apartheid and the Struggle for Palestine" they proclaim:

"We, South Africans who lived for decades under rulers with a colonial mentality, see Israeli occupation as a strange survival of colonialism in the 21st century. Only in Israel do we hear of 'settlements' and 'settlers.'

Only in Israel do soldiers and armed civilian groups take over hilltops, demolish homes, uproot trees and destroy crops, shell schools, churches and mosques, plunder water reserves, and block access to an indigenous population's freedom of movement and right to earn a living. These human rights violations were unacceptable in apartheid South Africa and are an affront to us in apartheid Israel."

On October 23, 2001, Ronnie Kasrils, a Jew and a minister in the South African government, co-authors the petition "Not in My Name." Some two hundred members of South Africa's Jewish community sign the statement because, "It becomes difficult, from a South African perspective, not to draw parallels with the oppression expressed by Palestinians under the hand of Israel and the oppression experienced in South Africa under apartheid rule."

Three years later, Kasrils goes to the Occupied Territories and concludes, "This is much worse than apartheid. Israeli measures, the brutality, make apartheid look like a picnic. We never had jets attacking our townships. We never had sieges that lasted month after month. We never had tanks destroying houses. We had armored vehicles and police using small arms to shoot people but not on this scale."

On April 29, 2002, while in Boston, South African Archbishop Desmond Tutu says he is "very deeply distressed" by what he observed in his recent visit to the Holy Land, adding, "It reminded me so much of what happened in South Africa. The humiliation of the Palestinians at checkpoints and roadblocks, suffering like us when young white police officers prevented us from moving about."

Referring to Americans, Tutu adds, "People are scared in this country to say wrong is wrong because the Jewish lobby is powerful—very powerful. Well, so what? The apartheid government was very powerful, but today it no longer exists."

In November 2005, I attended a lecture in Gainesville, Florida, given by two Anarchist's Against the Wall. Jonathon Pollak, an Israeli activist and organizer for Anarchist's Against the Wall, explained they are a collaborative NONVIOLENT resistance and civil disobedience group led by Palestinians but supported by Israelis and Internationals dedicated to bringing the separation wall down and ending the occupation of Palestine.

Pollak said, "Although Israel marketed the Wall as a security barrier, logic suggests such a barrier would be as short and straight as possible. Instead, it snakes deep inside the West Bank, resulting in a route that is twice as long as the Green Line, the internationally recognized border. Israel chose the Wall's path in order to dispossess Palestinians of the maximum land and water, to preserve as many Israeli settlements as possible, and to unilaterally determine a border.

"In order to build the Wall Israel is uprooting tens of thousands of ancient olive trees that for many Palestinians are also the last resource to provide food for their children. The Palestinian aspiration for an independent state is also threatened by the Wall, as it isolates villages from their mother cities and divides the West Bank into disconnected cantons [bantusans/ghettos].

"The Israeli human rights organization B'Tselem conservatively estimates that 500,000 Palestinians are negatively impacted by the Wall. We believe that, as with Apartheid South Africa, Americans have a vital role to play in ending Israeli occupation—by divesting from companies that support Israeli occupation, boycotting Israeli products, coming to Palestine as witnesses, or standing with Palestinians in nonviolent resistance."

I agree and I also know that Apartheid can be summed up as a structured process of gross human rights violations perpetrated against a conquered ethnic majority by a state and society mainly controlled by an invading ethnic minority and its descendants, mainly immigrants, which have been deemed part of the ethnic elite.

The following nine categories make up the necessary, sufficient, and defining characteristics of apartheid regimes:

1. Violence: Apartheid is a state of war initiated by a de facto invading ethnic minority, which at least in the short term originates from a non-neighboring locality. In all main instances

93

of apartheid most if not all members of the invading group originate from a different continent. The invading ethnic minority and its self-defined descendants then continue to dominate the indigenous majority by means of their military superiority and by their continuous threats and uses of violence.

2. Repopulation: Apartheid is also a continuation of depopulation and population transfer. One example is seen in the obliteration of the indigenous Bedouins that Israel denies free movement to graze their herds and are silently transferring the Bedouins to new locales, such as atop of garbage dumps.

3. Citizenship: The indigenous people are often denied citizenship in their own country by the apartheid state authorities, which are ironically and irrationally, run and staffed by the recent arrivals to the country.

4. Land: Apartheid entails land confiscation, land redistribution and forced removals, almost without exception to the benefit of the invading ethnic minority. Usually, members of the ethnic majority are forced on to barren and unfertile soils, where they must also try to survive under impoverished and overcrowded conditions.

5. Work: Apartheid displays systematic exploitation of the indigenous class in the production process and different pay or taxation for the same work.

6. Access: There is ethnically differentiated access to employment, food, water, health care, emergency services, clean air, and other needs, including the need for leisure activities, in each case ensuring superior access for the favored ethnic community.

7. Education: There are also different kinds of education offered and forced upon the different ethnic groups.

8. Language: A basic apartheid characteristic is the fact that only very few of the invaders and their descendants ever learn the language(s) of the indigenous victims.

9. Thought: Finally, apartheid contains ideologies or 'necessary illusions' in order to convince the privileged minorities that they are inherently superior and the indigenous majorities that they are inherently inferior.

Much of apartheid thought is shaped by typical war propaganda. The enemy is dehumanized by both sides' ideologies, words and other symbols are used to incite or provoke people to violence, but mostly so by the invaders and their descendants.

Minister of Intelligence in the South African Government, Ronnie Kasrils wrote how traveling through Palestine's West Bank and Gaza Strip, was "like a surreal trip back into an apartheid state of emergency. It is chilling to pass through the myriad checkpoints—more than 500 in the West Bank. They are controlled by heavily armed soldiers, youthful but grim, tensely watching every movement, fingers on the trigger . . . A journey from one West Bank town to another that could take 20 minutes by car now takes seven hours for Palestinians, with manifold indignities at the hands of teenage soldiers . . . The monstrous apartheid wall cuts off East Jerusalem . . . Bethlehem too is totally enclosed by the wall, with two gated entry points. The Israelis have added insult to injury by plastering the entrances with giant scenic posters welcoming tourists to Christ's birthplace."

The Wall or as Israel prefers to spin it as a 'security barrier', is designed to crush the human spirit as much as to enclose the Palestinians in ghettos. Like a reptile, it transforms its shape and cuts across agricultural lands as a steel-and-wire barrier, with watchtowers, ditches, patrol roads and alarm systems. At a height of 8m to 9m in places, it dwarfs the Berlin Wall. The purpose of the barrier becomes clearest in open country where the route cuts huge swathes into the West Bank to incorporate into Israel the Jewish settlements—some of which are huge towns and all are illegal under international law.

If The Wall is truly to keep out terrorists, why was it not built on Israeli land? Minister in the Presidency Essop Pahad, explained, "It has become abundantly clear that the wall and checkpoints are principally aimed at advancing the safety, convenience and comfort of settlers. The West Bank, once 22% of historic Palestine, has shrunk to perhaps 10% to 12% of living space for its inhabitants, and is split into several fragments, including the fertile Jordan Valley, which is a security preserve for Jewish settlers and the Israeli Defence Force. Like the Gaza Strip, the West Bank is effectively a hermetically sealed prison. Roads are barred to Palestinians and reserved for Jewish settlers. I try in vain to recall anything quite as obscene in apartheid South Africa."

On December 20, 2006, Archbishop Desmond Tutu, who received a Nobel Peace Prize for his relentless work confronting and challenging South Africa's Apartheid regime was quoted in The Guardian, "Israel will never get true security and safety through oppressing another people. A true peace can ultimately be built only on justice . . . If peace could come to South Africa, surely it can come to the Holy Land."

Justice requires equal human rights, liberty and self-determination for all people. Justice requires honoring International Law and the Declaration of Human Rights. The establishment of Israel's very statehood was contingent upon upholding the UN Universal Declaration of Human Rights and as a Member State, America is obligated to hold all other Member States to it.

The Declaration of the establishment of Israel promised, "On the day of the termination of the British mandate and on the strength of the United Nations General Assembly declare The State of Israel will be based on freedom, justice and peace as envisaged by the prophets of Israel it will ensure complete equality of social and political rights to all its inhabitants irrespective of religion it will guarantee freedom of religion [and] conscience and will be faithful to the Charter of the United Nations."—May 14, 1948

"IMAGINE all the people living life in peace."
—John Lennon

IMAGINE good and evil cut through every human heart.

IMAGINE that Free Will means we get to choose which rules.

IMAGINE leaders of the world being led to do the right things.

IMAGINE God smiling upon the dysfunctional family of Father Abraham when Israelis and Palestinians both enjoy equal human rights in alliance with international law.

IMAGINE God smiling upon America when our Founding Father's values are reflected in policies of today.

IMAGINE Conscience may just be another name for that Mystery we call God.

IMAGINE God does bless America and everyone else too!

SOURCES:

"Apartheid Ancient, Past, and Present Systematic and Gross Human Rights Violations in Graeco-Roman Egypt, South Africa, and Israel/Palestine" by Anthony Löwstedt

"Foreign Agents: The American Israel Public Affairs Committee from the 1963 Fulbright Hearings to the 2005 Espionage Scandal" by Grant F. Smith, Published 2007 by the Institute for Research: Middle Eastern Policy, Washington D.C.

"THE ATTACK ON THE LIBERTY: The Untold Story of Israel's Deadly 1967 Assault on a U.S. Spy Ship" by James Scott. Simon & Schuster, June 2009.

SPECIAL REPORT: THE STIKE ON THE USS LIBERTY, John Crewdson, Tribune Senior Correspondent, October 2, 2007

The Link, "About That Word Apartheid", April-May 2007, Published by Americans for Middle East Understanding, Inc.

Mail & Guardian, Israel 2007: Worse than Apartheid, by Ronnie Kasrils.

Washington Report on Middle East Affairs

http://ifamericansknew.org/

http://endtheoccupation.org/

EXPERIENCE!